Negotiations Without a Loser

Iwar Unt

Negotiations
Without a Loser

Copenhagen Business School Press
HANDELSHØJSKOLENS FORLAG

Negotiations Without a Loser

© *Copenhagen Business School Press*, 1999
Cover designed by Kontrapunkt
Cover photo: Spencer Rowel
Language consultant: Robert W. Goldsmith
Set in Plantin and Printed by AKA-Print, Denmark
1. edition 1999

ISBN 87-16-13460-5

This translation from Swedish to English is based on:
Iwar Unt, Lär dig förhandla! Liber-Hermods, Malmø 1995

Distribution:

Scandinavia
Munksgaard/DBK, Siljangade 2-8, P.O. Box 1731
DK-2300 Copenhagen S, Denmark
phone: +45 3269 7788, fax: +45 3269 7789

North America
Copenhagen Business School Press
Books International Inc.
P.O. Box 605
Herndon, VA 20172-0605, USA
phone: +1 703 661 1500, fax: +1 703 661 1501
E-mail: intpubmkt@aol.com

Rest of the World
Marston Book Services, P.O. Box 269
Abingdon, Oxfordshire, OX14 4YN, UK
phone: +44 (0) 1235 465500, fax: +44 (0) 1235 465555
E-mail Direct Customers: direct.order@marston.co.uk
E-mail Booksellers: trade.order@marston.co.uk

Preface

Negotiating is part of everyday life. You negotiate far more than you realize. In a business or an administrative position, you do so when you're dependent upon others for getting your ideas accepted, your goals accomplished or your problems solved. You also negotiate on how tasks, rights and responsibilities, resources and risks, expenses, and monetary gains and losses should be assigned or divided up.

There are two quite differing approaches you can take. One is that of a "zero-sum game." Here, whatever one party loses the other party gains. If you want more, this can only be achieved if the other party gets less. A zero-sum game is a battle with both a winner and a loser.

The other approach involves cooperation and the creating of a partner-like relationship. Negotiating requires an open and constructive discussion on how different solutions might affect everyone's total costs and total gains. Cooperation of this sort can create added value. It enables you to gain more without the other party having to lose, or to gain less.

My aim is to show you how cooperation of this sort can be achieved. This book is based on my experiences and impressions over the past 20 years working with people in administration and management – training them in the art of negotiation. Among my many long-term customers are leading Swedish and international firms, such as Alfa-Laval, ABB, Astra, Atlas-Copco, Bofors, Bonniers, Celsius, Electrolux, Ericsson, the Swedish Military Equipment Administration, IKEA, Kvaerner, Norsk Hydro, Philips, the Swedish Postal Services, Procordia, Saab-Scania, SEB Bank, Skandia, Telia, Trygg-Hansa, Trelleborg and Volvo.

I want to provide you with practical, useful knowledge you can apply on a day-to-day basis. I suggest no patent solutions. Every situation involving negotiation is unique. The solution called for in any given situation needs to be worked out in its own way. Each individual negotiator has to develop his own approach.

Life itself consists of a long series of negotiations. If you learn to negotiate more effectively, you will increase your ability to influence the things that happen, and to maintain control over your life.

Iwar Unt

Contents

Introduction

This is a book written for those who participate in negotiations or are responsible for their being conducted. I will concentrate on the roles of the buyer and the seller. However, this book also has much to offer those who participate in other ways. You may be a department head, a project leader, have a specialty of some kind, or whatever. In occupational contexts of widely differing sorts, negotiations are often an important part of your task. Whenever you are dependent on others for carrying out your job or for achieving your aims, you are often forced to negotiate.

Regardless of whether negotiations are internal to your organization, or external, involving other organizations or individuals, you are expected to behave in a professional and businesslike manner. It is imperative for you to arrive at rational solutions that are appropriate in terms of what is at stake and what is possible to achieve. Whatever your occupation, it is important for you to be good at negotiating.

To simplify the text, I make frequent use of the pronouns "he" and "him". These stand just as much for "she" and "her" as the other way around, and also just as much for "they" and "them" in referring to organizations or to groups of negotiators.

The book is divided into three main parts:

1. Negotiations from the standpoint of the buyer
2. Negotiations from the standpoint of the seller
3. Advice on how to negotiate.

Your role is that of a *buyer* when you are interested in some offer or suggestion that others have made, which you can either accept or reject. The aim of those you negotiate with is to sell you their ideas, their point of view, or their solution to a problem. They want you to accept what they propose.

You may be in the position of hiring a new employee who is asking for a salary that is too high. There may be a plan presented to you by colleagues who are convinced they have found solutions to certain problems that have long plagued the organization. Or your boss may have given you the task of meeting each of three job applicants and selecting the one who is best.

In contrast, you are in the role of a *seller* when you want to convince others of your point of view, your ideas or some solution you are arguing for. Here you want to gain the other party's cooperation and support, or their affirmative response. Your goal is to break down the other party's resistance.

For example, to get the go-ahead from your boss, you may need to convince him to "buy" your suggestions. To be hired for a new job, you may have to gain the confidence of your potential employer, selling him on the idea that you are competent. For your budget proposal to be accepted, you may need to demonstrate that it can be put into practice and that it is consistent with the goals of the organization. To obtain resources for a project, you may have to convince those higher up that the project would be worthwhile.

In thinking about these two separate roles you may have noticed that, as a negotiator, you can actually assume both roles. Considering a business deal in which the customer buys or receives goods, the seller also buys or receives business, as well as a share of the market. The seller may also gain competence through developing a new sales technique. The buyer, in turn, sells a portion of the market, as well as access to certain know-how and use of his organization's name as a reference.

In the two major sections that follow the first will deal with negotiations from the perspective of the buyer, while the second will consider that of the seller. Regardless of whether you identify primarily with the one perspective or the other, you should read both sections. Negotiating is a psychological contest between persons or parties, one in which rationality and logical reasoning are often pushed aside in favor of feelings and emotions, the actions of the other party often being difficult to comprehend. If you learn to consider negotiations from perspectives other than your own, then the irrational behavior of the opposing party, his inability to understand you, and the combativeness he displays, will become easier to understand.

The better your knowledge is of the mechanisms that steer the parties negotiating with each other, the more secure you will feel. When you are confident you negotiate more effectively, without any need to fight with the other party. It is only those who are insecure, ignorant, or uncertain, who resort to the law of the jungle.

I want to enable you to view negotiations as a cooperative undertaking, as a partnership in which you and the opposing party attempt constructively to find solutions that satisfy both your needs. Successful cooperation results in solutions that are more cost-effective and involve less risk. The needs of others and the needs of the environment are more likely to be given consideration. In general, greater overall value and profit can be created than is achievable in negotiations where both parties simply try to manipulate each other and fight until one or the other gives up.

We not only negotiate the best ways to solve problems while meeting the needs of both parties, but also how to divide up responsibilities and work, as well as the distribution of costs, risks, profits and gains. Accomplishing this successfully places special demands on you as a negotiator. You need to be businesslike. This requires your finding a happy balance between two extreme behaviors, that of being naive, and that of being greedy.

A naive negotiator gives away too many advantages and too much potential profit. He accepts too much of the work and responsibility, and too many of the risks. Thus, a naive negotiator is expensive for the organization. He is easily taken advantage of. Even the parties he negotiates for may have little trust in him.

A greedy negotiator wants to get everything without being willing to give. He is unable to accept the idea of the other party gaining anything. He wants to thrash the other party and defeat it. A greedy negotiator is also expensive for the organization. No one wants to deal with him. People avoid him if they can. Those he has victimized are likely to seek revenge. A greedy negotiator, just like the naive one, fails to gain trust and support.

My aim is to help you become more businesslike, to thus be neither greedy nor naive. I present the negotiation models neither as patent solutions to problems, nor as though they guaranteed a straight and simple road to successful negotiating. They are like scales or chords when you are learning to play the piano: they serve as a basis for developing your skills. Every round of negotiations will be unique. The opposing party will be unique as well. The more chords, scales and tempos you have in your repertoire, the better able you are to adapt your negotiating skills to the situation at hand.

A zero-sum-game approach versus creating added value

We will now consider in some detail the two basic approaches to negotiating referred to above: a zero-sum-game approach and a cooperative approach. It is not a matter of one approach being right and the other wrong, but rather of determining which combination of the two you should choose to achieve the best possible results. Through initial cooperation you can establish a good relationship with the other party and a mutual sense of trust. You can also create added value that both of you can benefit from. The zero-sum-game approach can then be used for dividing up between the two of you the added value that has been created.

At the same time, a cooperative approach places strong demands on both you and the other party. Most negotiators, lacking insight into the advantages this approach offers, have difficulties in getting it to function, and may even lack the motivation to do so. Thus, they fail to get the sort of open and constructive dialogue going that is necessary. When negotiations affect them emotionally, their rationality breaks down. Threatening circumstances, stress and a sense of insecurity lead to their fighting tooth and nail with the other party, or to their avoiding issues and running away. Such reactions are inborn, deeply anchored within us.

A zero-sum game approach, in contrast to the cooperative, is characterized from the very start by negotiations concerning how to divide up existing advantages, disadvantages, gains, losses, tasks and responsibilities. You negotiate about distributing what is there. The more one party gets, the less the other gets. The two parties are diametrically opposed. If this is the only approach you take, it is likely to result in one party considering itself the winner and the other the loser, or both parties losing.

Far too many negotiators consistently employ a zero-sum-game approach. Such negotiations tend to be characterized by bickering, manipulation, failure to listen, one-sided argumentation, uncertainty, distrust, and revenge seeking. Worst of all, no added value is created. Success at negotiating in this manner can cost more than it is worth.

It has been found that in the two-thirds or so of the cases in which negotiators end up reaching an agreement, they tend to be very poor at taking advantage of possibilities for creating added value. There is thus a huge neglected potential here for you to take advantage of and benefit from. You can utilize the added value you create without the other party needing to consider itself a loser.

Allow me to illustrate this. A buyer has been offered 10 computers, together with appropriate software, for $14,750. The offer includes delivery with software installed. The buyer then searches for similar competitive offers, but at a lower price, and demands that the seller reduce his price to just under $12,500. The bottom line for the seller, however, below which the price begins to hurt, is $12,875. Instead of simply reducing the price, the seller could ask himself: *what services or what additional equipment could we add to increase the value of the purchase for the buyer? If we offer five of the buyer's employees special courses in Word* (one of the programs included in the package), *what would that mean for us? We hold such courses every week. Our normal price is $187.50 for each participant. On the other hand, one or two spaces are usually empty. If we let the customer have them, it would not cost us anything.*

The seller offers the customer the possibility of sending 1-2 people a week to this course, provided space is available. The offer extends to a total of five people. Each of them is to get a 50 percent reduction, compared with the usual price for the course. Once offered, if the customer does not think five is enough, there is room to negotiate for a higher number of people. In addition, the customer can also be provided with larger monitors, or with other improvements in the hardware, all at a reduced price. If, at this point, the customer does not feel this represents any added value, he is obviously not interested in getting a larger package. What the seller could do, then, is offer to reduce what is included in the package, bringing down the price accordingly. The seller can suggest that the customer install the software himself, and also pick up the computers. Suppose this arrangement would save the seller $500 in labor costs. He can retain part of this, say $125, to increase the net value the sale would bring in, and reduce the price for the buyer by the remaining amount. If the customer does not agree to this, the seller could offer a price reduction against payment in advance, instead of the usual 30-day credit.

The buyer's perspective

Negotiations
from the standpoint of the buyer

We will run you through the various stages of purchasing negotiations as they develop from start to finish, showing step by step what strategies a buyer can take. To prepare for purchasing negotiations of your own, you can use the different headings and subheadings in this section as a checklist.

As a buyer, remember to maintain a businesslike approach. This requires that you do the following:

- Aim to achieve the lowest total costs possible in the agreement you arrive at. In comparing alternatives take into account any differences in opportunities for profit and risk. Price is only one of many aspects involved and is far from being the most important one.
- Reach an agreement that both parties will adhere to. Make sure that the supplier can fulfill the conditions specified in the contract.
- Establish a positive relationship with the supplier. After the conditions of the contract have been fulfilled, both parties should be interested in continuing the relationship.

A buyer who intends to take advantage of the supplier by use of power plays and rough competitive tactics, leading to a contract in which the supplier is forced to carry the most of costs and risks, all for a pitifully low price, is not behaving in a businesslike manner. In the final analysis such contracts often result in both parties losing.

Phase 1 – Sending a letter of invitation to prospective suppliers

The goal of Phase 1 is to prepare a letter of invitation that can serve as a basis for negotiations with a seller. The time you spend on this should reflect how important the purchase is to you. Factors to take into consideration are the amount of experience you have had with purchases of a similar sort, as well as whether it is simply the renewal of an earlier contract or a new one.

Clarifying your needs

What needs of yours will the goods or services involved fulfill? Will the purchase have any implications affecting your overall system or strategy, or is it to be a relatively simple purchase? If it is more than a simple isolated purchase, taking its overall affects into account will probably make negotiations more complex.

Example
You want to buy a spreadsheet program for your computer. The new program, which is a component of a larger system you already have, needs to be compatible with the existing hard- and software. Many people discover, after buying a new program, that it fails to function as it should, either because their computer does not have enough memory, or because they have an older version of certain other programs. Under such circumstances you can lose a lot of time and money, and become exasperated, just getting things to function properly. You can avoid this if you specify the environment the spreadsheet program would be placed in and get the salesperson to agree to take responsibility for making the program work. The problem is that many salesmen refuse to do this. This limits your search to companies that are willing to take on such responsibility.

A purchase can affect many people in your organization

A major purchase may have implications for a number of people in your organization, potentially affecting end-users, experts, and even service personnel, for example. Since such people may have considerable experience relevant to a given purchase, and special requirements, they represent a natural target group for suppliers, who often resort to *backdoor sales* methods in an effort to milk these people for all the information they can get.

Anyone at your place of work who is not particularly cautious may easily pass on information to suppliers which enables them to set prices advantageously and evaluate how competitive they are compared with other suppliers. Clever suppliers will go to great lengths to assess how valuable their products or services are to a particular customer, and how their position compares with that of their competitors. They base their prices not on their own costs plus a certain percentage added on as profit, but on the value their product has to the customer. Obviously, they try to get the highest price possible. Such an approach, which is termed market pricing, is surely used by your own marketing department as well. Just remember that it is to the seller's advantage to know how you rank them in relation to their competitors.

> **Example**
> "We're looking around for a new supplier right now. A replacement has been long awaited by those of us using our current ordering system. I'm sure that the impossibly long delivery times our customers have been faced with have cost us huge sums of money, but people just kept saying there wasn't any other supplier that was able to..."

This example illustrates what a backdoor seller might hear. One aim of backdoor selling is to commit you to technical solutions that give the supplier a monopoly. A clever supplier may entice your engineers by presenting them with exciting technology. Their engineers and yours often have much in common, both being interested in the development of more advanced technology, as well as having a common vocabulary, having attended the same schools and sharing many common values.

Since there are apt to be differences of interest between various departments and people in your organization, a coordinated effort is called for. It is important for everyone to reach an agreement before contacting suppliers so that you present a united front. A major purchase should be handled as a project with a project leader who is kept abreast of all contacts with suppliers. Before any meetings with any supplier, the project leader should be informed about who will be there, and of the goals that are to be achieved. He can decide when to schedule meetings with suppliers, or to delay if necessary, whether additional personnel should be present, and whether certain instructions should be given to those involved. The project leader should be immediately provided with the results of any such meetings.

Your assessment of the situation should include the following:

- An outline of your needs.
- The actions you are presently taking to satisfying those needs.
- A list of what you wish to buy, specifying primarily the functions to be fulfilled.
- A timetable for conducting negotiations, and for delivery of a purchase.
- An evaluation of what you would have real use for. What level of quality or performance do you need? If the speed limit is 110 km/hr, would you willingly pay for a car that could go 200 km/hr?

Determining your alternatives

If you lack choice, your negotiating position is weak. Having as many options available as possible helps you to arrive at optimal solutions. Opportunities for discovering new alternatives are limited only by the time you have available, your knowledge of the market, and the significance you attach to the matter in question.

It is therefore important to keep abreast of potential alternative suppliers and solutions. You should have a fairly good idea of what your current business partner can offer, but you may be somewhat limited by current agreements, solutions and conditions. Since you accepted the current prices and conditions, your present supplier can be expected to ask himself: *How much more is this customer willing to pay in the future? What reasons could I give for raising the price?* It is somewhat less likely that the supplier will ask himself: *How much do*

I need to improve my offer in order to keep this customer? Since a hungry supplier is more open to changing his approach than one who feels he's already "captured the prey," it cannot hurt to get your current supplier to reconsider the contractual terms that you agreed upon earlier. To this end, keeping yourself informed about what other suppliers offer will be quite useful. However, in order to help maintain a good working relationship, you might consider explaining to your current supplier that doing this is simply part of your job as a professional buyer.

> **Example**
> "People from a company called Technologic visited us last week. Are you familiar with them? No? They're competitors of yours. They sell a British system. Since what they offer is rather similar to yours, it could be an alternative for us, particularly from the standpoint of price."
>
> Avoid pretending. Do not risk your credibility by using fictitious competitors as threats. It is always counterproductive to threaten with something you neither intend to do, nor have any way of carrying out. The supplier may see through you.

Your assessment of alternative solutions and different suppliers should provide you with answers to the following questions:

• Which suppliers are available for you to turn to?
• What are the technical solutions that exist?
• What happens if you decide to just do nothing?

What experience from previous negotiations can you utilize here?

Despite your having gained experience from using various suppliers and solutions, you may have difficulties retrieving information on this. The information may be unorganized, or may never have been recorded. You should expect a negotiator to have kept records of previous negotiations in much the same way a physician keeps records on patients. Maintaining records of your own should allow you to see how the different firms and negotiators you have dealt with have be-

haved and reacted, and what individual or organizational characteristics they have displayed. Following is one example of records that a
seller might have on a buyer.

> **Example**
> Ned O. is a project leader in charge of purchasing services for his
> company. Andy H. is his boss.
>
> Ned worked as a salesperson for Ericsson Information Systems
> during 1981-86. He prefers being a buyer. He is an economist,
> educated at IHM. He has no technical training, which creates dif-
> ficulties if you try to discuss technical aspects in detail. Since this
> puts him at an obvious disadvantage, he does not like it, preferring
> to appear as if he can actually handle technical matters. It is there-
> fore best for you as a supplier to provide him with certain appro-
> priate written materials in advance so that he can prepare himself.
>
> He likes to make dramatic statements like, "If you raise your
> prices next year, that will sabotage our future contacts."
>
> If you as a supplier keep cool, not responding to such state-
> ments, he usually forgets having made them. He is difficult to
> work with. He will not open up and provide you with the whole
> story. He carries on like a poker player and I have never managed
> to see completely through him. Be sure to get things down in writ-
> ing. We have often failed to communicate with each other effec-
> tively. Sometimes I have taken his rash statements as promises.
> But one important element to remember in negotiating with him
> is to always give in on some point.
>
> He enjoys sailing and likes to talk about it. He drives a Vega.
> He is married to an English teacher, and they have two daughters.
> He is interested in politics and is an avid Social Democrat.

If you lack information about those you negotiate with, it is a good
idea to discuss things with colleagues and people you have contact
with at other companies. Also look into reports or results from product testing that may be relevant. As stated earlier, remember that the
strength of your negotiating position depends on knowing as much
as possible about the other party.

What is at stake in the negotiations at hand?

Your perspective should include a determination of the amount of
time and effort to be invested in particular negotiations, and in preparing for them. You should be able to answer the following questions:

- *What is it worth to you?*
  Not everything can be measured in monetary terms. There are
  many other considerations, such as the status and survival of your
  organization, protecting the environment, having sound information to base decisions on, being able to predict what will happen,
  and so forth. Time is also important, with short-term values needing to be weighed against long-term ones. Values should be expressed in a manner that can be readily grasped. You may feel too
  that you should measure them. At times, expressing them in dollars or in some other currency can be useful. At other times there
  may not be any such simple measure available. This can make answering the next question difficult.

- *How much should it be allowed to cost?*
  Here you should consider how valuable the matter is to you, what
  alternatives you have, what it would cost if you took care of the
  matter yourselves rather than letting the seller do it, and what the
  consequences would be if you did nothing at all. Another approach is to ask what costs the other party would have, what he
  would be risking, how much he would need to get in order to come
  to an agreement, and what alternatives he has.

- *What will you need to invest yourself?*
  What resources of yours will be required and how can this be incorporated into your overall calculations?

- *What is at stake for the other party?*
  To be able to judge the strength of your own position, you will also
  need to ask what the deal means to the other party. Consider such
  matters as monetary gain, employment, references, technology,
  market position and survival.

What resources of yours are involved?

What can you lay on the table to negotiate with? To get anything, you have to be willing to give something in return. Prepare yourself for the bargaining ahead and the search for added value. Aim to reduce the risk and total costs of the project, and to increase the overall value of its return. As a buyer, you can contribute to a project in many different ways. Resources you can provide may include the following:

- *Economic resources*
  All projects need to be financed. If you have sufficient resources to contribute toward financing the project and can provide advance payment, decide on the conditions under which you would be willing to do so. Two questions are important here, involving financial security and interest costs. Can the other party provide adequate security, such as a bank guarantee? If the supplier's interest costs are higher than yours, would your making an advance payment result in an overall value increase? It may be possible that if you took on part of the financing, it might reduce the total costs of the project, which could be of benefit to both of you.

  In your efforts to negotiate in such a way that added value can be achieved for both parties, there are a number of steps you should follow:

1. Identify those areas that are subject to negotiation.
2. Determine within what limits you can negotiate on a given matter.
3. Determine to what extent any changes in the conditions agreed to can be realized in a practical way.
4. Consider what such changes would mean both for you and the other party.
5. If added value can be achieved, take advantage of this and negotiate how it should be distributed between the two of you.

Example
A supplier wants to be paid within 30 days. You may be willing to make a payment in advance if the supplier provides a bank guarantee. Suppose that making a 40 % advance payment would cost you $12,500.

> "Are you interested in getting an advance payment?"
> "Of course."
> "Can you give us a bank guarantee?"
> "Certainly."
> "How much would you reduce the price by if you got an advance payment of 40%?"
> "By about $15,000."
> "That's not very much. If you could give us $17,500, we'd be able to go along with that."
> " Well, unfortunately it isn't worth that much to us. We can't go down by more than $15,625."
> "If you'll go down by $16,250, we'll give you the contract."
> " All right. But you're pressing me further than I ought to go."

- *Personnel resources*
  The usage of personnel resources in a common project with another company may indeed have important financial implications, but there will be many other serious considerations as well. For example, how well will your people hit it off with theirs? How much trust is there? How much insight do you have into the overall picture on both sides? To what extent do you believe in the project? Will there be any benefits from training that your personnel might receive?

- *Material resources*
  Consider whether and to what extent you can contribute to such matters as development, production, transportation, storage, maintenance and dismantling. Here, too, there may be relevant considerations beyond just the financial implications.

- *Time resources*
  Consider the importance of investing your own time and effort when making a purchase from a supplier. The more active you are as a buyer, and the more you help the supplier, the more rational and inexpensive purchases will be. You help yourself by helping the supplier.

It is unfortunate that many buyers seem unwilling to cooperate with suppliers in efforts to discover alternative solutions. Some buyers declare openly that such ideas need to come from suppliers, whose task they see as being that of not only selling, but of draining away financial resources. Buyers of this sort disclaim having any intention of helping a supplier.

Some buyers even refuse to discuss alternatives that suppliers come up with. They are entirely fixated on paying the lowest possible price. They take no account of the total costs involved. Although incompetence and insecurity may help explain such behavior, there is not justification for it in any business sense.

Preparing a letter of invitation

When you write a letter of invitation to prospective suppliers, bear in mind how you want negotiations to proceed. If an uncomplicated purchase is all that is involved, where you can easily specify what you want, and where quality and service are of no appreciable importance, it is certainly enough just to compare prices from different suppliers. If the amounts of money involved are small, you gain nothing by conducting lengthy negotiations. Negotiating by phone will probably suffice. Always assume, however, that any offers you get can be improved upon by negotiating.

Example
You plan to have something printed and you see no point in conducting negotiations on matters of volume, quality or completion time. You decide that whoever offers the lowest price will get the job. You have received three offers: A. $4,000, B. $4,949 and C. $5,949.

You phone up B, thank him for his offer, and ask if he is interested in the job. You explain that he is 20-30 percent more expensive than the competition. You ask why and whether he would be willing to come down in price. He says the other printers must be using a different type of machine, since they could not possibly do the job so cheaply otherwise. You conclude that the $250 reduction in price he would be willing to make is not sufficient. Thus, you do not award him the job. You have a similar conversation with C.

A, the printer that interests you most, is the one you phone up last. You ask how he plans to do the printing. He explains it. This confirms your impression that the printers simply differ in the techniques they utilize, which is why the prices vary so greatly. You then could discuss A's offer in any of three different ways:

1. By making a counter-offer, such as, "I'd be willing to pay you $3,695 for the job."
2. By asking, "Could you go through your computations again and see if there are any adjustments you could make in what it would cost?"
3. By bluffing, for example by saying, "Your offer is too expensive. See what you can do about the price."

Your telephone calls take 15 minutes, at the most, which provides your company with considerable savings for the time you have spent. If you had not questioned A's price at all, but had given him the job directly, he could easily have been disappointed and have wanted to kick himself for not having asked for more. He would be likely to raise his price next time.

Be conscious of the fact that, from the very the moment you make the first contact with a supplier, negotiations have begun. The supplier will do everything from that point on to steer you in the direction of solutions to things he has to offer. In all ensuing contacts he will also try to determine what your alternatives are, your price limits, and what the value is to you of what he has to offer.

A letter of invitation is a document with legal implications. It details how an offer is to be expressed, what specifications need to be met, what guarantees need to be provided, and how a contract should be formulated.

It should be noted, however, that such letters are susceptible to a multitude of interpretations. Since you cannot exclude this possibility, you should then follow up with a personal contact to ensure that both sides clearly understand each other.

Give the supplier as much freedom as possible and be open to any unexpected alternatives he may suggest. Avoid such statements as, "We're looking forward to receiving an offer from you at the lowest possible price." Remember that price is often not the only consideration. You should always look at the total cost a particular alternative would involve, and its overall profitability.

How many suppliers should you be in contact with? The greater the number, the more likely it is that you will find what you want, but the time and work involved will also increase. One basic principle to bear in mind is to always have more than one alternative, not just at the start, but throughout the negotiations, right up to the point when a contract is signed. Never stick to just one group of suppliers either. See to it that fresh blood comes in. Make your suppliers conscious of your being active and in contact with their competitors.

If you are in the public sector, there may be rules for competitive bidding that stipulate how your letter of invitation should be formulated and how to decide which supplier to use.

Summary of Phase 1 for the buyer

1. Assessing your needs.
- People affected – users, advisors, service personnel, etc.
- Needs you are faced with.
- Functions involved and possible solutions.
- Time schedule.
- Appropriate level of quality or performance.

2. Alternatives you have. Lacking alternatives weakens your position.
- Possible suppliers and solutions to choose between.
- What happens if you do nothing?

3. What information and experience of yours or others is available?
- Experience you have had previously with different suppliers and different alternatives.
- Draw on experience from colleagues.
- Use available test results and reports.

4. What is involved in satisfying your needs?
- Determine what it is worth to you and how much you can spend.
- Know to what extent you will be directly involved in the project.
- Find out what it is worth to the other party, financially and in terms of full employment, references, technological gains and market position.

5. Considering your own resources.
- Financial.
- Personnel.

- Technical.
- Time.

6. *Specifying in a letter of invitation the terms to be negotiated.*
- Complying with any competitive bidding rules that apply.
- Specifying demands to be placed on suppliers.

Phase 2 – Comparing offers on equal terms and preparing for negotiations

Your task as a buyer is to satisfy the needs of your organization at the lowest possible cost. Expressed differently, it is to help maximize your organization's financial gains. It is never simply to buy at the lowest possible price. In assessing alternatives, take into account your organization's needs and the demands you place on suppliers. If some of your demands are absolute, eliminate any supplier whose proposal fails to satisfy these particular demands. You then evaluate the desirability of the remaining alternatives that you have judged to be basically acceptable. You compare them on as equal terms as possible.

Evaluating offers

In evaluating the alternatives that different sellers propose, you need to analyze factors that influence the costs, profits and risks involved. This serves as a basis for comparison, as factors of this sort often interact. Opting for high quality, for example, although costing more initially, can result in lower operating costs, more reliable operations, increased overall value and greater protection of the environment.

The optimal way to determine which solution is best is to take into account all relevant factors involved and how they interrelate. This would, however, require a huge investment of time, access to large computer capacity and making use of complex mathematical models. If your selection task is to be manageable, it should remain somewhat simplified, for example by only considering factors that have a direct effect on the desirability of the alternatives, and be readily measured or assessed. Consider how these factors affect matters of costs, overall profitability and the like. This means translating the effect of each factor into the same measure, such as US dollars, for example.

Example
Although buying a product of higher quality should mean it will last longer, say 15 years instead of 10, you should ask how long your investment in the product will actually be useful to you. Advances in technology or changes in the market might mean the product's usefulness would last only five years. High quality would then be of no practical value in this respect.

A high quality product could, however, reduce maintenance costs. If such a reduction amounted to $12,500 per year and the product had an economic life for your company of five years, this would increase its total value by $62,500.

The complexity of assessing the merits of various alternatives and suppliers leads many buyers to opt for an easy way out. All they look at is the price, simply noting that $150,000 is $12,500 less than $162,500.

To adequately compare alternatives, you may need more information than you have immediate access to. In a simple case, printed materials may be sufficient, or you may need to request written clarification. In a more complex situation, negotiations may become necessary. Many suppliers are reluctant to provide detailed information on technical aspects of their products, being afraid that their competitors will get hold of it. They maintain a low profile initially, not revealing any more information than is necessary. They are interested in the biggest slice of your pie, but are reluctant to share anything they have before bargaining has begun.

One final point to be conscious of is the fact that many purchasing decisions are based more on emotionally colored judgments than on facts. Try to keep this in mind, especially if you find yourself becoming friendlier with certain sellers. Other sellers that you personally find less to your liking socially may in fact have better products or services to offer your company.

What opportunities do you have for negotiation?

Concentrate on factors that will affect the overall outcome, and compare the alternatives in terms of total costs involved. Remember that it should be clear to yourself in advance just what is negotiable on your part, i.e. on what points you will be open to accepting certain changes. These are changes that can affect cost, risk or profit. As an example, suppose you are willing to be flexible on the following matters:

Payment arrangements: You could agree to make an advance payment.
Delivery times: You would prefer faster delivery, since this would enable you to begin production sooner.
Service: You could consider making a service agreement with the supplier.

After this, you will need to determine how flexible you can be, and in what areas, as well as how much flexibility you will expect from the supplier:

Payment arrangements: You would be prepared to make an advance payment of up to 50 percent.
Delivery times: Since getting ready to start the production will take at least six months, there is nothing to gain from an earlier delivery, though you are likely to suffer a loss if delivery is late.
Service: You would be willing to sign a service agreement of up to five years.

After determining your degree of flexibility, the next problem to anticipate will be the effects such changes might have on you. Would your costs rise or be reduced? Would your gross receipts increase? Would the risk you are exposed to decrease? Attempt if possible to express such consequences in monetary terms:

Payment arrangements: Making an advance payment costs you something and involves risk. If making an advance payment of 50 percent means paying the seller $200,000, plus taking out a 30-day loan for this amount based on 10 percent per annum interest charges, your interest costs would be $ 1,667.
Delivery times: In the event of a late delivery, you have calculated that each month you have to wait beyond the first agreed upon six months will cost you $12,500.
Service: A service contract with an outside organization would cost you $25,000 a year. You consider this to be the most that a service agreement with the supplier should cost.

A negotiating scheme helps you keep track of things

In preparing for negotiations, there are usually a considerable number of issues to be analyzed. You should attempt to achieve an overall view of things so that you know where you are free to negotiate, how much leeway you have, and what the negative consequences will be if you fail to gain agreement on various issues. You should also be conscious of how your negotiating position as a whole will be affected if you get less or more in regard to some point. Maintaining a clear picture at all times of everything that is going on is important, since this will enable you to discover ways in which added value can be achieved and how it could be divided up. Keeping track of things by using a scheme will also help you play an active role in discussions and maintain the initiative.

Steps involved in preparing a negotiating scheme

The following steps can be suggested:

1. Make a *list of every possible issue* you think might come up, such as deadlines, price, performance, guarantees, payment schedules, hardware, software and questions of volume or numbers of items. Include not only issues dealt with already in the offer, but other issues that may be relevant. This could include the possibility of renting rather than purchasing, the value of the product if it is sold at a later date, trade-in values, service aspects not previously covered in the offer, installation, maintenance, and training of personnel.

2. To further assist in determining how much *leeway you might have to negotiate with,* you should consider whether there is anything you can make use of that is not already mentioned in the offer. Also consider whether you get by if you fail to get everything. This will also help indicate how much flexibility you have and what alternative solutions you could accept.

3. Consider the *consequences of changes in the terms* you argued for initially. This will keep in the front of your mind issues that are sensitive from your standpoint, separating those that could have severe monetary consequences from those that would have little such effect.

4. Try to obtain an impression of the *leeway the supplier has* in negotiations on different issues. Does he have any alternatives you have not thought of?

5. Try to gain an understanding of *how the supplier would be affected* by any changes in the initial terms. Although it is difficult to form a complete picture of things, having as much information as possible will make it easier for you to discover variables that can be utilized to produce added value.

Most of us have an unreliable memory when dealing with the multitude of figures that can be important in the course of negotiations. This is another reason why a good negotiating scheme is a necessary tool for negotiating. The following is an illustration of what a negotiating scheme might look like:

Variable	*Offer*	*Flexibility*	*Value*
Payment arrangements	100% upon delivery	We can provide an advance payment of 50% if a bank guarantee is provided.	Our costs are 10%/year of the outstanding sum. 50% costs $1,667.
Delivery arrangements	April 1, 2000	Nov. 1, 1999 at the earliest	Each month is worth $12,500.
Service	Option	The longest period we can sign a service contract for is five years.	We can pay up to $25,000 a year for full service.

To determine where potential areas of negotiation lie, i.e. areas in which added value can be achieved, the information given above would need to be complemented with similar information concerning the supplier's situation.

What opportunities does the seller have for negotiation?

Look carefully at the negotiating scheme to find points where you feel the supplier could take a flexible approach. Try to determine how far he would be willing to go and what consequences various changes would have for him. This helps reveal where added value can be achieved. Added value is created when appropriate changes in the conditions agreed on can be made, and when any of the following conditions are met:

• Your costs in taking on the extra task or responsibility in question are less than his would be.
• The extra profits you would get are greater than the added costs would be for the supplier.
• Both of you would gain a profit.

Consider the following case:

Payment conditions: The supplier's interest costs are 8 percent, whereas yours are 10 percent. Thus, your making an advance payment would provide no added value.

Delivery time: For each earlier month you are able to start due to earlier delivery, your earnings will increase by $12,500. Being able to start three months earlier would thus put you $37,500 ahead. Assume that delivering the goods three months earlier would cost the supplier $15,000 extra. Under these conditions, the added value attained would be the difference between the two: $22,500.

Service agreement: The supplier offers you a one-year service agreement for $22,200 but is willing to reduce this to $18,750 a year if you opt for a five-year agreement, for which you would pay $93,750 altogether (5 X $18,750). Suppose the best independent alternative you can find would cost you $25,000 a year, and thus $125,000 over a five-year period. Agreeing to the supplier's offer would result, therefore, in a value increase of $31,250 ($125,000 - $93,750).

Now the problem is how to get your hands on this kind of useful information. The most obvious approach would be to ask the supplier to specify what he would be willing to add to what he has offered already. You could do this either directly during negotiations or in informal contacts.

It is important to ask in the right manner so that you do not give yourself away. Your questions may contain information that reveals more than it should. For example, you might signal a readiness to pay for a faster delivery time by asking, "Can you provide delivery earlier than specified in your offer, and if so, what would that cost?". The supplier would then try to find out how much this would be worth to you, and would demand a portion of your added value, whether or not he incurs any added costs. (Under "Phase 3 – Strategy," we will consider in detail how the result you achieve is affected by how you express yourself.)

You are now in a position to complement the negotiating scheme presented earlier, adding two new columns to it.

Variable	Offer	Flexbility	Value	Flexibility of the seller	Value to the seller

Analyze the situation the seller is faced with

Negotiations are a game played between at least two parties. It is thus important for you to have thorough knowledge about the other parties involved. Since it is always people who negotiate, not the companies or organizations they represent, you also need to know as much as possible about the person you will be dealing with. What is his position in the organization? What options has he been given? Which other individuals will be there?

You should take into account any cultural aspects that might affect the situation. This does not go so far as to mean having to speak a foreign language or knowing what foods, if any, are a religious taboo for the person you meet. However, do keep in mind that numerous different cultures often exist alongside each other in the same country. Even within your own country, there will be a wide variety of cultural differences, such as those between technicians and economists or between the public and the private sectors.

Another problem sellers face, as mentioned earlier, is the attitude of the buyers themselves. I sometimes hear people argue, "Since we're the ones who buy, it's the suppliers that need to adjust to us!" Why? You negotiate with suppliers in the hopes of being able to satisfy your needs, which improves your own situation. This means you are dependent on them.

Also be alert to avoiding cultural clashes by being highly perceptive and adjusting to the situation. This will help facilitate communication on both sides and create a sense of openness, trust and mutual understanding. Try to imagine what the situation is like for the other party. What needs and goals does he have? What are his strengths and weaknesses? How might he respond to the moves you make? What position might a certain move put you in, and where would you go from there? There is no way, of course, to prepare for every possible event, or to consider all possible alternatives. Reality is full of surprises. Suppose your plan falls apart and the supplier takes a completely different approach than you had counted on. What should you do then? Simply admit to yourself that you are involved in negotiations that you did not properly prepare for. Recognize that any new signals or information you receive may alter your position completely. Take a break so that you can return to the negotiations with a fresh point of view.

Just as you made a rundown of your own checklist, make a rundown of your supplier's checklist as well. By viewing negotiations from a different perspective, you gain greater insight into the possibilities at hand and any resistance the seller is likely to put up. Make use of radial thinking, a technique I describe in the section entitled "Negotiations from the standpoint of the seller."

In summary, analyzing the seller's situation provides you with insight into what you can offer him as a step toward achieving your own goals. Negotiations are a give and take proposition for everyone, so avoid falling into the trap of simply trying to force your demands or of resorting to threats. Developing cooperation, openness and trust is the best way to create added value.

With whom should you negotiate?

After evaluating various offers you will end up with a number of suppliers that you want to take a closer look at. In what order should you meet them?

Many buyers opt for negotiating last with the supplier they believe in most, considering their negotiations with the others largely as dress rehearsals for the real performance. This provides you a means of improving ideas and arguments before presenting them to the anticipated choice of supplier. This supplier is thus afforded the opportunity to outbid the others.

Other buyers prefer parallel negotiations, partly to save time and partly to raise the temperature of the negotiations. They make it clear to each supplier that they are inviting them to serious discussions, but that negotiations are also underway with one or more of their competitors.

How should you deal with the information, technical solutions and offers provided by different suppliers? Should you maintain complete discretion and neutrality or should you inform other suppliers about offers made by competitors? Views on what is morally and ethically correct differ. Some buyers consider it their moral responsibility to exploit competition to the maximum. They believe that if supplier A has presented them with a particular technical solution to a problem, they should inform other suppliers about it, giving them a chance to "compete under the same conditions." They feel that if a supplier wants a proposal kept secret, he should request it.

Other buyers feel that if a supplier has invested time and resources coming up with a solution, and they possess the necessary know-how and creativity, they should be rewarded by making them the sole source for that particular solution. Such buyers consider theft of know-how to be short-sighted, since it could endanger relationships with first-rate suppliers, who might then refrain from providing any further offers.

Another shortcoming to passing on information from one supplier to another is that suppliers who attempt to copy the ideas of competitors are likely to lack the experience needed to exploit them adequately, so that nothing is accomplished. Furthermore, a buyer who spreads sensitive information in this way can easily be regarded as unreliable, since suppliers can then say, "If my competitors' secrets are passed on to me, won't mine be passed on to them?"

The approach you select will affect your relationship with suppliers. This is not a choice between black and white. Neither approach is always right or always wrong. The rules and principles differ from one supplier or situation to the next. The competitive bidding principles that apply in the EU, for example, include a clause prohibiting the leaking of trade secrets. Violations can lead to heavy fines.

Some buyers solve the problem by commissioning a preliminary study of the market. They are free to use what they have found out, since it has been paid for.

In dealing with suppliers, you should use the degree of discretion you feel is best, given the situation at hand. Ask yourself whether you want the negotiations to assume more the character of a cooperative endeavor or of a contest.

Examples
The following two cases illustrate how a particular message can be communicated in two very different ways. In negotiating, you are more often faced with the question of which way to move, rather than of whether or not to move at all.

> "You've suggested that we use a concrete framework, but we'd like you to consider a different alternative, which would be to use a steel framework. We've heard that using steel would make the factory a lot cheaper to build. Could you give us a rough sketch of how it would look if that were how it was built? We'd also like to know how this would affect building costs, the time you'd need to finish it, future maintenance costs, how long it would last and what sort of insurance premiums we'd be paying."

> "We've gotten drawings and estimates from a competitor of yours showing that it would be entirely feasible to use a steel framework for building our factory. We'll give you a copy of the material we got from them so that you can work out an alternative price."

What to think of before negotiations begin

In any meeting in which you negotiate, you should have a definite *goal*. There may be a long process involved, with many decisions along the way, before things are concluded. You should have some *alternative goal* to fall back on if you fail to achieve your major goal.

Intentional delays

Many negotiators are not result-oriented. This makes for long, drawn out negotiations, often with no result in the end. Such negotiators can become very much pressed for time. If an agreement is reached, they may feel they have been forced into making a poor decision. Time pressure may cause both negotiators to lower their goals. Such negotiation may do more harm than good.

On the other hand, you may consciously use a strategy of delay. Creating time pressure is a well-known way of getting the other party to agree. If he is more intent on reaching an agreement than you are, this puts him at a psychological disadvantage. He may then end up reducing his margins or profit simply to meet the deadline.

Example

Toward the end of May, the buyer contacts a market analyst to hear whether he has the time or interest in conducting a market research project. The project is slated for late August. Early in June, the two of them meet to discuss details. The market analyst provides the buyer with an offer and tries to persuade him to reach a decision. The buyer claims it is now in the hands of a steering group that has not yet given him a go-ahead. However, the buyer emphatically states, "The project is going to come off." The buyer then asks, "If you get a confirmation from us by late summer, could you start at the end of August or early September?"

The customer replies that such an arrangement should work out all right. At the beginning of August, still not having heard anything from the buyer, the market analyst phones to find out whether the decision has been made. He is told that the steering group is going to try to decide on the matter within a week. A week goes by, no further contact. He waits three more days, then phones the buyer again.

The buyer begins by saying:

> "We'll try to get started on the matter now. Do you still have the possibility of carrying out the investigation at the beginning of September?"
> "Yes, I've done my best to keep this time open for you."
> "That's fine! But we still haven't discussed the price."
> "But I already gave you an offer back in the beginning of June."
> "That's true, but the price you gave us is too high. We haven't reserved that much in the budget and here are others we've had contact with who are less expensive. You want $13,750, but we can't pay more than $8,750."

The market analyst has been caught napping. He had figured on getting the job. If he does not get it, he may have nothing else for several weeks. His negotiating position is very weak. He is faced with a choice between the devil and deep blue sea. Realizing that $8,750 is better than nothing, he accepts the buyer's offer.

How smart this buyer seems to have been!

But what happens now? The market analyst feels tricked. It is quite natural for someone who has been cheated to seek revenge. He will have no desire to obtain further work from this buyer. The buyer, on the other hand, who is in need of a well-conducted study, ends up with a mediocre analysis. The report leaves more questions open than it answers. In fact, it is so vague, it cannot serve as a reasonable basis for decisions. Yes, but it was cheap!

Where should negotiations take place?

Choose an appropriate place to meet for negotiations. Being at your home base can give you a sense of security. You also save time, have better access to expertise and documents, and you do not have to travel anywhere. It also makes it easier for you to take the initiative.

At the same time, being at their place would allow you to delay proceedings by indicating that there are certain important documents or information you do not have. There is also the opportunity you will have while there of gaining an impression of the supplier's production capacity, to what extent the capacity is used, and how much they have in stock. You may also get to meet various people of interest who are not taking part in the negotiations.

Having an agenda

You should always have an agenda. It can be either one of internal character, for your own use and not to be revealed to the seller, or one you work out with the seller beforehand. The latter will allow the seller to prepare, thus being better able to answer questions and make decisions.

On the other hand, if your aim is to avoid engaging in constructive discussions with the seller, you may wish to employ the element of surprise, for example by introducing an agenda that "knocks the legs out from under him." To avoid being faced with such a situation yourself, as well as to better prepare yourself, you can ask the seller to send suggestions for an agenda.

Assigning roles to different members of your negotiating team

If the matters you are to take up are sufficiently important to economically justify bringing in available personnel, you should have a team of negotiators to help representing you. In selecting those who are to participate, you should assign each an appropriate role. It may be too difficult for a single negotiator to not only lead the discussion, but also listen to what others say, observe what goes on, assimilate new information, analyze what has been said, keep track of new angles that appear and be an expert in the various areas involved. However, negotiating as a group will be difficult if the group lacks discipline and the roles assigned are unclear. A group can only have one leader.

The traditional division of roles between a chief negotiator, a technical expert, an economic advisor, and a lawyer, etc. is often not very satisfactory. The chief negotiator has a role somewhat analogous to that of an orchestra conductor. He takes the initiative in discussions, speaks for the group, makes decisions, and determines when other members should be brought into the discussion. He should assign the following supportive roles to other members of the group:

- *A listener,* whose main task is to listen to what is being said, observe what is going on and take detailed notes. During pauses in the proceedings, this person should be able to summarize for the others what has happened, what openings have appeared, how he feels the seller has reacted, what signals he feels the seller is trying to convey, and to what extent negotiations are proceeding as planned. Since the listener concentrates simply on listening and observing, he is in a much better position than anyone else in the group to form an accurate picture of how things are proceeding.
- *An evaluator,* who quickly digests new information that comes up and analyzes what it means, how it can be utilized, what economic implications it has and what solutions to the problem it suggests. This person is basically a navigator.
- *An alternative discussion leader,* who can take over as discussion leader when the need arises, giving the chief negotiator time to

think, to digest information, or simply focus on listening to and observing the seller.

Each of these people can have a double or multiple role, such as being an expert in one or more of the areas involved. However, it is the chief negotiator who calls upon each of the others in whatever role is required when the need arises. It is also he who makes all the important decisions.

Members should also agree in advance on how to communicate with each other. They should know how to warn the others if they realize that the chief negotiator is having difficulties, that he has missed a signal or that he is headed for a trap. Members may decide that, when this happens, they will send notes to each other, kick each other under the table, whisper in each others' ears, suggest taking a break, say, "Just a minute! I don't agree," or whatever.

Before going from one question to the next, the leader might also turn to the group and ask, "Do any of you have any thoughts or questions you'd like to express? Can we go on? Are we able to make a decision now or should we take a break?" This will allow the others to get in on the act in an appropriate way.

Bringing in external expertise

Since the knowledge and experience available within the organization may not suffice in all cases, external expertise may be called for. Experts may need to be hired in to solve technical problems, to provide advice on how to conduct business in some foreign country, or to obtain answers to various legal questions. Remember that the best time for getting advice from lawyers and other experts is before you sign a contract.

Summary of Phase 2 for the buyer

1. Evaluating different offers.
- What factors should be taken into account? What costs, possible gains and risks are there?
- Consider how these factors affect your overall profitability.
- Analyze and compare the different alternatives.
- Is more information needed? How can you get hold of it?

2. What opportunities for negotiating do you have?
- What factors are there for which you can accept a change in terms?
- What are your limits? How far can you go?
- What consequences would a change in terms have for you?
- A negotiating scheme helps you keep track of things.

3. What opportunities for negotiating does the seller have?
- What factors are there for which he might be willing to accept a change in terms?
- What are his limits? How far can he go?
- What consequences would a change in terms have for him?
- Is it best to find this out through negotiations or by informal contacts?

4. What sort of situation is the seller faced with?
- Who are you negotiating with? What authority does he have? Who makes decisions there?
- What cultural characteristics does the other party have?
- What goals and needs does he have? What are his strengths and weaknesses? What arguments can you use?
- How will he negotiate? Go through his checklist, or at least the one you imagine that he's using.
- What can you give him in return so that you can better achieve your own goals? (See point 3 above.)

5. With which suppliers should you negotiate, and how can this best be done?
- In what order should you meet different suppliers?
- What information should you reveal to them about other offers you have received?
- Is your strategy clear? What approach to bargaining should you take? What should you be ready to give in order to get what you want?

6. What should you think of before beginning to negotiate?
- What is your goal? What subordinate goals and alternative goals do you have?
- What time factors are there? What deadlines does the other party have? Avoid being put under time pressure.

- Where should negotiations take place? Have you worked out an agenda?
- Have you selected other participants to be in your group? What roles have they been assigned?
- Do you need external expertise? Get what legal advice you need before signing a contract.
- What are the legal principles that might apply in the event of a dispute? Is any license or permit required?

Be prepared to take the initiative in negotiations, analyzing the added value that can be achieved.

Phase 3 – Strategy

Negotiations can be conducted in many different ways. No single method can be said to be the best in any absolute sense. Situations differ so much that any attempt to find the ideal method is pointless. Just think of the differences there can be in the goals people set. Whereas some negotiators have blind faith in competition and the role of power, others regard cooperation as the best approach. The six-stage approach described below is an example of how negotiations might be conducted effectively if your aim is to optimize economic advantages, maintain good relations with the other party, and sign contracts that satisfy both parties.

Requesting a new offer

If you feel negotiations will work out best by taking a hard line from the start, you can begin by asking the other party for a new offer. Emphasize the existence of strong competition and that you want your discussions to continue, but indicate that his offer does not measure up to your expectations. Be prepared to provide an answer if the supplier responds by saying "Why? What are you dissatisfied with?" Do not bluff by claiming that there are others who are asking a much lower price or who provide more. Such a statement could be easy to verify, reducing your credibility.

The aim of emphasizing the competitive nature of a situation is to make the supplier insecure. If he has demanded a rather high price, your request is likely to make him uncertain of how competitive his offer is. This can be expected to make the supplier more willing to reduce his margins in order to "buy" a spot in the final round of negotiations.

Be conscious, however, of the fact that such an opening can place a burden on negotiations, making them more difficult to conduct and perhaps resulting in your getting nowhere. Everything depends on whether the supplier finds you and your claim credible. An experienced supplier may ask himself: "If my offer is really that bad, why is the customer continuing to negotiate with me? Is he continuing because other suppliers' offers are less attractive than mine? Does it mean that the customer has no other alternative than turning to me?"

An experienced supplier might make concessions of the sort you request but then place other demands on you in compensation. A tough but less experienced supplier might test his strength by saying that he had already made the best offer possible. The less the supplier believes in you and what you have claimed, the greater the risk that negotiations will come to a standstill.

Before making either of the moves just described, which could lead to negotiations becoming blocked, you should first try to figure out what you can do to keep negotiations going. If other equally good suppliers are available, you should negotiate with them as well. This will genuinely provide you with a basis for saying to the first party, "Your offer doesn't measure up to our expectations." If you have no other suppliers that are just as good, you need to get yourself out of the deadlock in some other way. The following methods can help:

- *Offering something in return:* "Let's try to solve the problem in a different way. What can we do to help you? If we made an advanced payment of 30 percent, how much could you come down in price?"
- *Delaying:* "Take a careful look at the things I'm asking for. Don't put yourself under any time pressure. We can arrange for a new meeting."
- *Signaling your readiness to compromise:* "Don't regard this as an ultimate demand on our part. I'm sure you can improve your offer enough so that we can reach a compromise that's acceptable to both of us."

The risk of your reaching a dead end increases if you offer a price that is obviously too low, if you fail to explain what it is you are dissatisfied with, or if you do not make it clear why you are continuing negotiations.

Examples

"Thanks for your offer. I realize you've made a real effort to meet our demands and to see to it that we're satisfied. We appreciate what you've done and we would like to continue the negotiations. My feeling is that we can establish a sound basis for working together, provided we can overcome certain difficulties. Your greatest problem, as I see it, is that the competition among suppliers has become so tough. We need to ask you, therefore, to reconsider your offer and take account of a number of things. One is that the delivery time is too long. We'd like to have it shortened by three weeks. At the price we'd be paying, we also feel that full service should be included the first year. An even tougher point is that we'd ask you to reconsider your price generally. If you can do something for us in these respects, we feel it would be sensible for us to continue negotiations."

"Actually, I don't know just why we called you here. The price you gave us shows that you don't have much contact with the market or with the realities of the situation. However, since you're here, we'll give you a chance to present a new offer."

Using a more cautious opening, you could attempt to make the supplier uncertain by asking him to understand your situation. You can argue, for example, "Our budget isn't sufficient for that." Or, "The top brass has said 'no'."

One purpose for using a tough opening is to gain a psychological advantage. If the other party gives in, he shows both that he is very interested and that he is uncertain whether his offer is sufficiently attractive. He may also give in because he would prefer doing business with you than with certain other companies, despite the demands you are making.

You need to be careful, however, to not lure a weak or inexperienced supplier into a business deal that gives him no profit at all, or that turns out to be more than he can manage. Experience shows that anyone who bends over backwards to please, getting nothing in return, will often go even further and give away most of the leeway they would otherwise have in negotiations. You should not lose sight of the need to preserve the economic potential of the other party and its desire and ability to fulfill the contract.

What may seem to be a success in negotiations can quickly change into a costly failure. What sort of situation will you end up with if the product is not delivered on time, is not of the right quality, if production breaks down or if the supplier goes bankrupt? How will you get service and spare parts under such conditions? The list of problems can be immense.

You can generally assume that an initial offer is one that is open to negotiation. A business deal is neither made nor broken by a supplier failing to get all his demands. There are implicit margins built in that allow the party to give in if necessary. There is, nevertheless, a risk that you may demand too much, giving the other party a signal that you are planning to make a real controversy of things. This can result in your ending up in a deadlock.

Even if the supplier does have a certain amount of latitude in what he is able to offer, he may not opt to use it. If you and the supplier are too far apart, or if the supplier does not like the way he is being treated, he may decide to give up the idea of having you as a customer.

Begin looking for opportunities to achieve added value

Just as you can regard an initial offer as being open to negotiation, you should also assume that any solution that has been suggested is open to improvement. Look here for opportunities to achieve added value, which can be created in various ways. Five of these are described below.

Through sharing the costs or responsibility for a project

This approach is appropriate if your costs are lower than those of the other party. There are costs that may come about at many different stages of a project, such as in connection with development, construction, production, storage, transportation, installation, maintenance, financing, purchase or disposal after breakdown.

Suppose the supplier has offered you payment on 30 days credit. You offer him, in turn, advance payment if he will lower the price. If advance payment will cost you $2,500 and the supplier offers you a rebate of $3,750, for paying in advance, an added value of $1,250 has been created. I will return later to how added value can be divided up between the two parties.

Through letting delivery be coordinated with deliveries to other customers

If a product is designed to satisfy the needs of various customers, the costs of developing it can be spread out over several different customers. Such a product is also likely to be produced in large series, lowering the costs per unit.

Let us say, for example, that you have requested delivery in August. If, instead, you can allow postponement of delivery until November, your order can be produced together with an order for another customer. If postponing delivery in this way costs you $12,500, whereas the savings in production costs amounts to $50,000, an added value of $37,500 has been created.

Through improving the product

It may be that the product can be improved by increasing its life expectancy, decreasing its maintenance costs, or increasing its residual value. You could also make it more environmentally friendly and perhaps available to a greater number of users, or you could reduce transportation and storage costs. The second-hand value of a machine would also increase if its quality were improved. For example, a machine might cost $25,000 more than the machine the buyer planned to buy originally, but have a second-hand value that is $62,500 higher than the other one.

Through exploiting differences between you and the other party in readiness to take risks

You plan to engage a well-known singer for a concert. Although it would be theoretically possible to sell 10,000 tickets at $6 apiece (giving you proceeds of $60,000), it would be risky to count on selling more than 4,000 tickets (which would give you proceeds of only $24,000). In view of the $25,000 fee the singer is asking for, it appears that things might not work out, since this would mean a loss of $1,000 (ignore here the costs of renting the concert hall, which we will assume are covered by a grant from the city).

Since the singer is convinced there will be virtually a full house, and that you would thus be taking in far more than she is being paid, she does not want to reduce her fee. However, by perhaps offering her a set fee of $15,000 together with 50 percent of the proceeds from the sale of tickets 4,001 to 10,000, you might get her to agree. This is because she could then expect to gain $33,000 altogether (6,000 X $6 = $36,000 X .5 = $18,000 + $15,000 = $33,000), well above the set fee of $25,000 she wanted originally. Thus, she may be willing to reduce her set fee, believing as she does in there being a full house.

This would allow you to avoid the risk of financial loss from paying what you feel was too high a set fee. The singer thus accepts the risk of selling too few tickets.

Through clearing up potential misconceptions

> **Example**
> The buyer demands, "If you want it to be a deal, you'll have to give us a guarantee for a much longer period than the one year you've offered us."
> "The one-year guarantee we've offered you is completely in line with what's usual in this branch. Neither we nor any of our competitors provide a longer guarantee than that."
> "Then there's no deal."
> "There's no point in your threatening us. We're simply following what's customary here."

The seller's mistake was to simply reject what the buyer wanted, viewing it as a threat rather than as a chance to be exploited. The buyer's mistake was to not be more explicit regarding what he meant by a more comprehensive guarantee. In such one-way communication both parties run the risk of not getting through to each other. The misunderstandings that came about here could have been cleared up if the seller had learned to respond to a customer's demands by listening and asking questions.

> **Example**
> "When you speak of a more comprehensive guarantee, what exactly are you looking for?"
> "We expect you to look after the machines over the next five years to ensure that they continue functioning properly."

"Is it a service agreement you'd like?"
"Yes."

Added value is more likely to be created during a relaxed discussion of alternative solutions to price, usefulness or profitability. If added value is achieved, both parties can have their needs fulfilled, with two winners instead of one. By aiming at increasing the overall value, both parties can also contribute, in the last analysis, to an increase in prosperity for society in general. The strategy this involves is what I refer to as a cooperative endeavor or partnership. There are two basic reasons why cooperation of this kind leads to better results:

• The openness involved leads to more information being available when decisions have to be made. This allows you to see solutions you would have missed if you only had access to the information already at your disposal.
• When two parties cooperate, there are synergy effects. If both parties share their knowledge and experience, an increase in value will come about. Both of you can perceive and exploit possibilities you might easily have neglected if you had tried to solve these problems alone.

What is required for cooperation to take place

The major requirements that need to be met in order for a cooperative approach to function properly are the following:

1. The parties must trust each other sufficiently to be open. Communication needs to be both ways.
2. Both parties need to believe that a cooperative approach will provide better solutions than competition.
3. Both parties need to be rational and well informed so they can adequately judge the practicality of any changes to the terms of agreement, and recognize any gains or savings that might be achieved.
4. There has to be a certain degree of generosity on both sides, each party allowing the other to take advantage of part of the added value that has been created. A party that tries to take everything will never be able to establish any long-term cooperation.

However, many buyers are afraid to work in this manner. They feel that such signals of cooperation could be misunderstood as weakness. They therefore start off negotiations with a tough approach, informing the seller that his offer is unacceptable. This is done in order to place the seller in a weakened position where he is more likely to give concessions.

Although this approach is risky, the risk can be reduced if you begin in the following way:

"I hope you'll understand that we're not prepared to accept this offer in its present form. The overall price needs to be reduced by at least ten percent. We also think your offer would be more attractive if we renegotiated the payment arrangements and time of delivery, and if you provided us with a service agreement. We've also given competitors of yours a similar opportunity."

Before discussing with the other party how an overall value increase can be achieved, you should analyze the situation and determine the following:

• Variables in your offer that you would be willing to change. Ask yourself whether you could get by with less, or whether you could do certain things yourself instead of having the other party do them for you. Determine whether it might be best to have an outside party take over part of the work and responsibility.
• Variables not considered in the original offer that need to be addressed.
• Which variables are not open at the moment to possible change, and why.
• How factors that hinder discussion of these variables could be overcome.

Gaining insight into the seller's situation and his manner of thinking

Remember to take the initiative in negotiations by asking questions and summarizing what has been said. A necessary condition for getting answers, however, is for the seller to trust you. He must feel negotiations are being conducted in a spirit of cooperation, and be convinced that both of you are trying to discover added value to be shared. If you have battled with him earlier, he may be afraid to open up. He will avoid what he thinks are efforts on your part to get concessions while giving nothing in return. He may become suspicious, too, if he feels you are pumping him for information, being afraid you may pass on what he says to competitors. If you want to create a balance in this exchange of information and provide evidence for the honesty of your intentions, begin by opening up yourself. Give the seller new information of some sort. This helps create a positive atmosphere.

Example

"We're willing to entrust you with the job if our discussions result in a solution that reduces our costs by at least 10 percent. That should be possible if you are willing to change the terms of the agreement somewhat. For our part, we could possibly delete some of the requirements we included in our letter of invitation. How much could you come down in price if we make an advanced payment of 30 percent?"

"We could come down by between $7,500 and $8,750."
"That doesn't sound like very much. I had figured on something like $10,500."
"We couldn't go that far, but we could perhaps come down by as much as $9,500."
"We'll come back then to the payment arrangements when we present you an offer of our own. What delivery time would suit you best?"
"Would delivery before summer be satisfactory?"
"That sounds basically okay. What advantages would that have for you?"
"We'd avoid having to wait over the summer to be paid."
"How would this affect the price?"
"We'd have to consider that."
"Okay, let's go on. We could imagine installing it ourselves if this meant a sizeable reduction in price."

The information you get here is:

• The value which a change in the terms of agreement has for the other party

- What you get in exchange if you accept a change in terms that benefits the other party.

All of this should be seen in relation to your costs, risks and profits. If you find that the changes are feasible, and if your calculations indicate that they will result in a net gain, then you have discovered added value. If such is the case, you should include these changes in the contractual terms of your counter-offer.

Clarify how the added value achieved should be divided up

Who should get the added value that will be created? This depends on how negotiations are conducted.

Suppose that your business conditions change after receiving offers from different sellers in response to your initial letter of invitation. You now find it would be very much to your advantage if the delivery time could be shortened by up to three months, each month thus saved being worth $25,000 to you. How should you go about convincing one of these suppliers to shorten his delivery time? The following are five alternatives for how a buyer might go about this.

Alternative 1
The open and naive buyer

Example

"The delivery time is important to us. We'd like you to shorten it."

"It's possible we could do that, but it would cost you more, since that would mean extra work on our part. How much would it be worth to you?"

"As much as $25,000 a month. That's why we want you to do everything you can to make it possible."

"When do you want us to deliver it?"

"Three months earlier if you can."

This buyer has expressed the wish for earlier delivery and has emphasized how important it is. The seller has responded by saying that this would cost more. The buyer accepts this and says it would be worth

$25,000 a month. The seller can basically interpret this as the buyer being willing to pay $25,000 a month extra for this to be done. The seller might then ask for time to consider the matter, and when he returns say that shortening the time by three months would raise the price by $62,500 to cover the cost of overtime.

Note that a negotiator who simply lays all his cards on the table runs the risk of not receiving any of the added value that is created. What would have happened if the buyer had stated instead that shortening the time would be worth $12,500 a month, or half the amount mentioned above? Would the extra amount the seller responded with have been only half the amount it was? How open should the buyer be in providing information?

An even bigger mistake would be if the buyer implied that he was willing to pay $25,000 a month. The seller might then test to see whether the buyer would be willing to pay even more:

Example
"We still have some calculations to do. We could, I'm sure, reduce the delivery time by three months, but we don't have all the information we need yet to be able to say how much the price would have to be increased. As it looks now, we'd have to increase it by between about $80,000 and $90,000."

Alternative 2
The open and businesslike buyer

To retain a reasonable part of the added value an earlier delivery would provide, as opposed to giving it all to the seller, the buyer could say he is negotiating with other suppliers as well.

Example
"We're giving you the same chance to shorten the delivery time that we've offered your competitors. Several of them have said they'd be able to give us a delivery time three months shorter than you've offered. Having it shortened that much would put us ahead quite a bit economically. Giving us a delivery time as short as that would definitely increase your chances of receiving the order. Each month you could shorten it would be worth $25,000 to us."

This forces the seller to take competitors into account. Since he cannot be sure what others will be able to offer in terms of delivery time and price, he is less likely to raise the price much compared with what the faster delivery time would cost. This tends to discourage him from simply trying to grab as large a chunk of the added value as possible.

Although it may appear that this approach differs only slightly from that which the buyer might have taken with the first alternative, the difference in how negotiations continue can be considerable. It was important here that the buyer was honest about how much he stood to gain from earlier delivery, allowing the seller the chance to weigh this amount against what he would be out of pocket for shortening the time. Yet despite the seller being told that shortening the time was worth $25,000 a month to the buyer, knowing that competitors were involved prevented him from trying to take the lion's share of it.

If the buyer had said nothing about how much he stood to gain from the delivery time being shortened, the danger would exist for the seller to either underestimate or overestimate the monetary gain involved:

- If the seller underestimated the gain in value involved, he might make no efforts to shorten the delivery time. Suppose it would have cost the seller $6,250 for each month he shortened the time. Compare that with the $25,000 gain the buyer will have for each month the time is shortened. Not shortening the time would thus result in the failure to create an added value of $56,250 ($25,000 - $6,250 = $18,750 per month X 3 months), a value the two parties could have divided up between them.

- If the seller overestimated the economic gain the buyer would have through the delivery time being shortened, he might decide to spend more money on this than it was worth. Suppose it would actually cost the seller $37,500 for each month the time was shortened. That would be more than the buyer would stand to gain. Shortening the time by three months would thus result in a net loss in value of $37,500 ($25,000 - $37,500 = -$12,500 X 3). Had the seller known the added value, he might have been able to work out a counter-offer that still would have been to your mutual benefit, though perhaps the earliest delivery would have to be two months ahead, or something similar.

An experienced seller, to be sure, would scarcely fall into either of these traps but would approach you about the importance of the shorter delivery time before making his offer.

Thus, under some conditions, being open and laying your cards on the table is the best approach. Just avoid being naive.

Alternative 3
The cautious buyer who either does not dare
play with open cards, or does not know how

A poorly prepared buyer who is uncertain of himself often makes somewhat vague statements, sending out signals that can easily be misunderstood.

- "See whether you can do anything to shorten the delivery time and, if so, what extra costs you'd incur."
  Why add, "what extra costs you'd incur"? There might be no costs for the supplier at all. Let sleeping dogs lie.
- "If you're interested in giving us a shorter delivery time, we're open to suggestions."
  Well, why would anyone speed up delivery for no particular reason at all? You may need to point out that providing an earlier delivery could increase the value of the project. If this is not made clear, why should the supplier consider assuming the expenses of faster delivery? To prevent such miscommunication, you should always provide some incentive for shortening the time.
- "We want to give you the same opportunity to consider a shortening of the delivery time that we're giving your competitors. A shorter delivery time could be interesting for both of us."
  Here, too, you are providing the seller with no clear signal of what a value increase could mean to him.

The cautiousness shown in each of these remarks reflects uncertainty on the buyer's part regarding how open he can be without going too far. If he fails to lay his cards on the table, there is a risk that the seller will misunderstand what he means and make the wrong decision. Unless he calls any added value to the seller's attention, the latter is likely to consider what the seller is saying and the extra costs involved as negative.

Many negotiators have a hard time being open and frank in what they say. They fail to distinguish properly between what it means to be naive, to be businesslike and to be greedy. Keep in mind that greed will destroy any spirit of openness or creativity.

Alternative 4
Indicating to the other party
what you would be satisfied with

Suppose that, for the supplier, price is of utmost importance. If he does not know what you are willing to pay, he may feel unsure about offering a price. Suppose that for you, on the other hand, the deciding factor is not price as such, but whether you end up getting what you need without paying more than necessary.

Example
You are in need of a computer, along with certain accessories. What you want is a PC with a particular level of power and performance, a laser printer that also conforms to your expectations, and both a word-processing and a spreadsheet program thrown in. Looking at what is available, you see that such a package would cost you about $5,000. This is an amount you feel you could earn back within a short period of time.

There are three suppliers you have confidence in, so you decide to take a close look at what they have to offer. You ask each of them whether they would be able to sell you a package of the sort you are looking for at this price. All of them say they could. You tell each of them there are two other suppliers involved, and who you go with will depend on the additional features you are able to get.

You continue by saying:

"I'd find it valuable to have the programs installed, the machine delivered to my door, and to get several hours of training in how to use the programs. I'd also like the computer to have extra capacity, and some additional programs as well, such as graphics."

What do you gain from this? What is important to you is not so much the price as what you get for your money. The supplier can reason as follows: "How much would it cost us to install the programs and deliver to his doorstep? Can we afford to let him attend the courses he wants? We do sometimes have space free in our courses. It wouldn't cost us anything if we let him attend under such conditions. As far as the extra capacity he wants, we could install one of the cards the manufacturer gave us for demonstration purposes. This should do the trick."

The buyer was concerned about looking after his own interests and taking advantage of the added value he could get. The supplier, in turn, considered what the marginal costs would be of providing him with what he wanted.

Alternative 5
Preparing a contract that provides special incentives for keeping costs down

Suppose that, as matters now stand, the community is responsible for garbage collection and maintains thorough, ongoing information on the amounts to be collected and the costs. Assume too that the community is considering letting a private contractor take over, with the aim of cutting costs. The offer made to private contractors can stipulate that, to get the job, a contractor would have to reduce the costs to the community by at least 10 percent. It can be agreed that, if the contractor is able to reduce costs even further, both parties will receive an equal share of what is saved. A principle of open reporting of costs will be followed.

Summarize the results of negotiations and consider the matter carefully

It is still too early to finalize an agreement. Before you can do that, consider the various alternatives again carefully. Also, summarize the results of the negotiations, making sure that you and the other party have not misunderstood each other. After that, take a break. If this does not suffice, ask the suppliers you are negotiating with to submit revised proposals. Consider the following questions carefully:

- *Do you want a new round of negotiations?*
  Are the alternatives involved directly comparable? Have all puzzling aspects been dealt with adequately? Have all major questions been thoroughly explored? Is there time available to continue? Would a new round of negotiations be worthwhile?
  If you decide to go through a new round of negotiations involving all or some of the suppliers, what information should you give them? Should you conduct negotiations with them parallel to one another? Should you use some sort of auctioning procedure? Should they be given access to each others' proposals?

- *If you have already selected a supplier, should you give him a new proposal to test how far he is willing to go?*
  If so, should you indicate, at the moment you present the proposal, your readiness to compromise? A better approach might be to simply say, "That looks good, but we'd like you to take a careful look at it again before you present us your final proposal".

- *If you have already selected a supplier, should you create a sense of uncertainty nevertheless by delaying?*
  If time is on your side and the supplier seems uncertain and anxious to finish things off, he may be willing to go a little bit further toward meeting your requests. If your original goals have been achieved, should you go ahead and accept the proposal as it stands, or should you go on to see whether even more can be achieved?

- *If you have achieved your original goals and have decided to accept the supplier's offer, what should you do now?*
  Try to imagine how things will be in the future and to what extent you will have to deal with this same supplier later. Will you be buying from him again, establishing closer ties? Will he be providing you with continued service, where you will be buying spare parts from him, or he will be buying back the product in a used state? Request the option of buying from him again under the same terms as before, but without any obligation to actually do so. Such

an option should help protect you against unreasonable or exorbitant practices on the seller's part. If you do not have such an option, the supplier may be able to dictate terms later by having gained a partial monopoly in supplying you. Negotiate such an option while your negotiating position is still strong.

Complete the final details of negotiations

Although contracts made orally are just as binding as those made in writing, be careful to confirm in writing any agreements that have been reached. This allows any possible misunderstandings to be cleared up before it is too late. If things fail to work out later, the agreement you reached will have been documented on paper.

It is best that you formulate the contract yourself. The seller has the responsibility of contacting you then if he has a different view from what you have agreed upon. This also averts the danger of your being misled by statements in small print that you do not understand.

Analyze, summarize and document what has taken place in your negotiations with the seller. This will also be useful in any future negotiations with that seller. You may even conclude that a different approach will be more productive. Keep close tabs on how the project develops, contacting the supplier as soon as you discover or suspect there is something that should be changed or renegotiated, or if it is just not working out.

Contact the other suppliers to tell them who got the contract and the reasons. If you want to maintain a relationship with them for future competitive situations that you may wish to take advantage of, you should let them know the ways in which you feel their offer could have been improved. This is important, because they may otherwise feel cheated out of a contract. Though disappointed, most suppliers will appreciate your being open and providing them with objective and factual information on your decision.

Summary of Phase 3 for the buyer

1. *Asking for a new offer.*
- Point out the competition.
- Indicate that their offer does not measure up to your expectations.

- Create uncertainty by asking them to understand your situation and the fact that their price is too high.

2. *Searching for added value.*
   (Sometimes it is better to skip step 1 and begin here.)
- What variables does their offer contain that are open to discussion?
- What additional variables should be discussed?
- Why are some variables seemingly closed to discussion?
- How can this be changed?

3. *Gaining insight into the seller's situation and his line of reasoning regarding the price.*
- What would various changes in the terms of the contract be worth to him?
- If you agree to such changes, what will you get in return?

4. *Clarifying how potential increases in value should be divided up.*
- How much information about your own situation should you provide?
- Should you give the other party an extra incentive?
- How can you best distinguish between being naive, being businesslike and being greedy?
- Should you establish some lower limit to what the seller would need to offer in order for you to accept?

5. *When asking to be provided with a new offer, ask yourself the following questions:*
- Should you have a new round of negotiations with the other suppliers?
- Should you make a counterproposal to test how far a given supplier will go?
- Should you attempt to create uncertainty by a strategy of delay?
- If you have achieved your original goals, is it better for you to accept the offer in its present form or to see whether you can get more?
- What options regarding future business with the supplier should you ask for?

6. Completing the final details of negotiations.
- Confirming all agreements by means of a formal contract. It is you who should formulate it.
- Analyzing, summarizing and documenting the negotiations that have been carried out. Profit from the experience you have gained.
- Informing the other suppliers who got the contract and why.

The seller's perspective

Negotiations from the standpoint of the seller

We will now look at the negotiations you will be involved in as a seller, from the beginning to the end. At each stage, we will consider which strategy is best. When you are actually preparing to negotiate, you can use the various headings and subheadings in this text as a checklist.

As a seller, it is of course just as important for you to be businesslike as it is for a buyer. Being businesslike involves the following:

- Providing the buyer the greatest value possible at a price he regards as competitive, compared with what others are offering him. Do not "sell" just the price. Show the buyer what else he will get. Do not end up, on the other hand, sacrificing more of your profit margin than you have to for him to feel that the contract he is getting is good enough to be renewed.
- Being sure you can meet the obligations the contract involves. Say "no" to any contract outside the limits of what you feel you can accept.
- Creating a good relationship with the buyer and gaining his confidence.
- Discovering and exploiting possibilities for creating added value.

Sellers who aim simply at short-term profits and making a killing at the expense of the customer, who draw up contracts in which they promise more than they can hold, or who try to manipulate customers into making ill-considered decisions, cannot be taken seriously.

Phase 1 – Seeing the potential for making a sale

Your efforts should be directed primarily at those opportunities that appear most likely to succeed. Suppose you have received a letter of invitation, or that you have discovered some opportunity on your own that could result in a sale. To be able to judge whether making an offer would be worthwhile, there is a considerable amount you need to know.

View the matter in its entirety

One mistake many sellers make is to immediately become immersed in details. Instead of reflecting on whether they should submit an offer at all, they concentrate on the ins and outs of what the buyer wrote in his letter of invitation. Failing to see things in a broader perspective, they end up presenting an offer without having investigated adequately whether it would even be desirable to make one, or exactly what kind of offer they should make.

Consider how things are at the moment. Is the buyer looking for something new or for something he has bought from you earlier? If he has bought from you before, will he want the same product or service as last time, or some other solution? What other suppliers has he used in the past? Is there reason to believe he wants an offer simply to compare it with another one he is contemplating? Is he looking for improvements on what you provided before? Does the letter of invitation indicate his needs, problems or goals? Does the customer know exactly what he wants, or is he simply looking for information?

The fact that a buyer has taken the initiative to ask for an offer can be a very advantageous situation for you. The buyer has a problem and appears anxious to find a solution. Take advantage of this, but be sure to get as much information as possible from him before making an offer.

If you are responsible for making the initial contact, the situation is more difficult. You are in the position of being anxious to get somewhere, and it is up to you to awaken the buyer's interest. If he is perfectly satisfied with things as they are, it may take considerable time before your efforts lead to a sale. The problems you are faced with are:

- Knowing the right information about your product you should present to convince the buyer that your offer is something he needs and can benefit from.
- Gaining his attention so he will even listen.
- Making him sufficiently interested in continuing discussions with you.
- Collecting the information about the customer's needs.
- Gaining his trust.

Make personal contact with the buyer

It can be difficult to interpret a letter of invitation, however detailed and well prepared it may be. Something that means a particular thing to one person may mean something quite different to another. For example, the letter of invitation might state the following:

- *We need delivery at the latest by October 15th*
  Does "need delivery" actually mean that this delivery date is non-negotiable, or simply that the customer would "like to have" delivery by then? If it cannot be negotiated, why not? If it is something that is open to discussion, would October 30th be satisfactory instead? How much flexibility is there regarding the delivery date? What would the consequences be for the buyer of an earlier or later delivery?

- *We want it delivered by October 15th*
  Similarly, does "want" mean that the time of delivery can be negotiated or that delivery by that time is required?

This illustrates how easy it is to present your offer in a way that fails to take advantage of potential benefits for both you and the customer. By meeting with the customer personally, you can obtain information to help you avoid this. Your offer should have a human touch.

Business deals are made by people. Decisions are based just as much on your having close personal contact with the buyer as on your being able to present the best technical solutions possible at the lowest price obtainable.

Example
A study was published in 1994 on what bank directors consider to be most important in deciding whether to approve loans. The bank directors who participated were to indicate which of the following three criteria was most important:

1. That the customer be financially sound and able to provide security for the loan.
2. That the customer be able to present a realistic plan for how the loan was to be used.
3. Other considerations.

Most of the bank directors regarded the third alternative as most important, explaining this by saying more or less the following: "What's most important to me is to feel I can trust the person who wants the loan, and that we communicate well with each other. Matters of security on the loan and how the loan is to be used should be discussed, but are not of primary concern."

If you do not know the customer personally, visit him to introduce yourself. Aim at establishing close personal contact, at creating a sense of trust, and at knowing more about who he is and what he may be in need of. Other questions to address may be:

- Is he open to other alternatives and, if so, what kind?
- How are decisions made? Who does the buying? Who would the users be? Are you even negotiating with the right person?
- Why did he send you a letter of invitation? Does he genuinely regard you as a potential supplier, as simply a source of information, or as a means for negotiating a better deal with another supplier?
- What issues referred to in his letter of invitation will carry the most weight? Is he more interested in a low price or in what he will get for his money? How much is he willing to pay?

Analyze your competition and the buyer's alternatives

Before presenting an offer and becoming involved in bargaining, you should assess your strengths and weaknesses. It is important that you keep track of what your competitors have to offer, and that you be able to answer questions of the following type:

- Which competitors can present offers as good as yours?
- Which competitors can provide solutions other than yours to the same problems?
- Does the customer have other needs that will affect how much financing he has available for making a purchase from you?
- Does the customer have the option of postponing his decision?
- Does he have the option of not purchasing at all?

Analyze your own position

What role would a sale of this sort have in terms of your overall strategy? How important is it for you to succeed in making this sale? How much effort should you invest in it?

In answering these questions, you should consider the following matters:

- *Your needs*
  What are you looking for primarily? Is it maintaining jobs for your employees, achieving as high a market share as possible, entering new markets, or developing new products and services? How much money is involved? Do you have to keep within a certain budget?

- *Your goals*
  Be sure that you have established a clear goal before you negotiate. What are you trying to accomplish? Do not let your goals collide. Establish definite priorities.

- *Your resources*
  Are your economic, technical and personnel resources sufficient for you to take on this job, and will doing so fit in with your time schedule? If not, forget about it.

- *Possible alternatives*
  What alternatives do you have to taking on this job, and how good are they? Are there other customers you should focus more on winning instead? If you have no other alternatives, your position is weak. It increases the risk that you will give in to the customer's demands without daring to test whether you can negotiate.

- *Costs and risks involved*
  Is there a sensible relationship between the time you would need to prepare an offer and the profit you can expect? Are there other projects that might suffer if you invest time in this? Do you risk giving away know-how when you negotiate? Think of how it would be if all the customer really wants is to obtain your know-how, planning to then carry out the project himself, or go to a competitor of yours.

Legal aspects

What laws apply to the buyer? If he is within the public sector or if EU rules apply, for example, he may be bound to seek out competitive offers. It is important for you to know of any such legal rules that apply.

Summary of Phase 1 for the seller

1. *Look at the matter in its entirety.*
- Take a careful look at details.
- What is the customer doing at the moment?
- Are you clear about the customer's needs and goals?
- How is the situation affected by whether you made contact first or the customer?

2. *Make personal contact with the customer.*
- What is he actually demanding, as opposed to what he would simply like to have?
- Give your offer a human touch.
- Is he open to considering different alternatives?
- How are decisions in his organization made?
- Why were you sent a letter of invitation?

3. Analyze your competition.
- Which competitors are able to offer something equally attractive?
- Which competitors can provide alternative solutions?
- What other needs or interests of the customer compete for the resources necessary for what he wants from you?
- Can the customer simply postpone making any decision on the matter?
- Can the customer decide to not purchase from anyone?

4. Analyze your own situation.
- What are your own needs and goals.
- How adequate are your resources for providing what would be needed.
- What are your costs, risks and profits.

5. Legal aspects.

Phase 2 – Choosing a strategy before making an offer

Before making an offer, consider carefully what strategy would be best for the case at hand. The strategy you choose will effect negotiations. Note that one strategy can be combined with another, and that a strategy that worked before may not be the only one or the best one to use here.

Making a minimum price offer

A minimum price offer is the simplest solution conceivable, even if you know it will not meet the customer's needs, and that better alternatives are available. So why not offer the best you have immediately? This could be for any of the following reasons:

- Some customers are so fixated on price that they think of nothing else when choosing a supplier. Later, once you have your foot in the door and negotiations are underway, you may be able to get him to see matters from a larger financial picture.
- Some customers have difficulties translating the added value you offer into concrete advantages. In such cases a minimum price offer may help you to at least getting your foot in the door. After this you will have more opportunities to explain things, helping the buyer to see things from a broader perspective. So, if you are running out of time and you want to make sure you will have another opportunity to explain matters, make a low-priced offer. Besides, it may simply be that he is unable to take advantage of the higher quality or better product you have to offer.
- If there is not much you can offer in terms of technical advantages, a low price may be your best or only chance.
- If your potential for making a profit lies in your being able to complement your original offer with added features, an initial low price offer might be a good strategy for keeping you in the game. Later, when negotiating any changes or additions, many of your

competitors will at least be out of the picture. Your main aim is to get your foot in the door and getting the customer interested so that you can continue with negotiations.

- If you need to protect your own know-how, this could preclude presenting your best solutions to the customer initially. You know there is a risk otherwise that information about your offer may leak out to competitors.

Example

An ad attracts your interest: High-powered computer, Pentium III, 450 MHz for only $1,250!

You go into the store and begin discussing things with the salesman. He asks what features you would like the machine to have and puts together a package offer that includes all of them. The price ends up being $3,950. You do not consider this to be particularly expensive, considering everything you will get. In talking with the salesman, he succeeded in getting you interested in a computer with more features than you had planned on originally. The salesman won your confidence and you decided to go ahead and buy it.

How would you have reacted if the ad had stated the following instead? *High-powered computer, Pentium III, 450 MHz for only $3,950!* You probably would have gone elsewhere.

Hold off making an offer. Getting the customer to consider some alternative other than what he had originally thought of

Waiting to make your offer can be sensible if you have gotten the customer interested, and you feel there is enough time to get him to consider alternatives.

Such a strategy can be appropriate if:

- The letter of invitation is geared toward what your competitors can offer, but not to what you are able to offer.
- The customer is looking for something that will not really meet his needs best. You realize that both of you would gain if you can get him to accept your offer.

Using a preliminary study as a basis for making a sale

Sometimes, neither you nor the customer can determine straightaway how his needs can best be met. It may be unclear what the customer's needs are, or which needs should be prioritized. It may be best to consider a purchase within the context of a variety of different activities the customer is engaged in. It may also be that the technology the customer has access to will not suffice to allow a reasonable decision to be made.

Under such conditions, conducting some sort of preliminary study may be sensible. Such a study can allow you to get your foot in the door so you can then steer the customer toward some special alternatives you have to offer, and that perhaps only you can provide. Your contacts with the customer while such a study is going on can also help to establish a sense of trust, while becoming acquainted with various key persons in the customer's organization. In addition, the study may provide insight, indicating how the customer evaluates various aspects of the alternatives you can offer. It also makes it easier for you to discover added value for both of you, and to gather information on the various alternatives the customer has available.

If the customer invests money in a collaborative study with you, he is not likely to pay out additional funds for carrying out a study of this sort with someone else. If you succeed in selling him on the idea of this collaboration, it will put you well ahead of your competitors.

Example

A customer plans to order a computer program that is tailor-made to fit his needs and is to be integrated into the hardware and software system he already has. He specifies what he wants the program to do and the environment in which it will be placed.

A consultant who has received a letter of invitation points out that the customer's needs could be met in a number of different ways. He asks the customer the following questions:

- Is it planned for the system to be expanded sometime in the future?

- Have matters of security been considered? As things are now, it does not include access codes, which means unauthorized personnel can enter the system.

The consultant notes that some of the functions the customer wants may be expensive, requiring certain hardware to be added to the system. The consultant also notes that there is information missing in the letter of invitation, making it impossible to prepare an adequate statement regarding cost and time schedule. He suggests that the customer make a more thorough inventory of his needs. This way, he could be provided with a considerably safer and more flexible system at only a slightly higher cost. He recommends that a preliminary study be carried out to obtain the information needed for developing an appropriate system, a study he could offer for $7,500. He emphasizes that this is a very small amount compared with the investment of some $375,000 that development of the new system itself would involve.

The customer expresses the desire to share the costs of the study with the seller on a 50/50 basis. The consultant accepts, but requests a clause in the agreement stating that, if the customer decides to break things off after the preliminary study is completed, the customer is to pay $5,000 for the work. The customer accepts. The consultant is now in an appreciably better position for later negotiations than he would have been if the customer had entered into negotiations from the start not only with him, but also with competitors of his who, like him, had responded to the letter of invitation.

Making an offer that is completely in line with the letter of invitation

In many situations, it may be best if the offer you make conforms to the stipulations in the letter of invitation, particularly in situations such as the following:

- When making competitive offers for public contracts. Otherwise, there is considerable risk that your offer will be bypassed, the contract-giver having no obligation to give you a chance. His job may be simply to evaluate the different offers that have been submitted in terms of what the letter of invitation has stipulated. It may even be forbidden for him to choose an offer involving any form of alternative solution.

- When the buyer has gone to great lengths in the letter of invitation to specify what he wants. Here there is the considerable risk that any offer deviating from this will be rejected. You will always have the possibility at some later point to suggest other solutions that might be better, but you need first to get negotiations underway.

Giving the customer alternatives to choose between

You can always give the customer alternatives to choose between, while at the same time providing an offer that conforms to the specifications in the letter of invitation. If you do not provide such alternatives, there is the danger that you will end up competing on the basis of price only. A list of options can be submitted, encompassing a choice involving higher and lower quality and performance. Such alternatives can make it easier for you to get to the negotiating table, and make you more competitive.

Ask yourself the following, however: At what point in the course of negotiations will you profit most from revealing the alternatives you can offer? It may be good to have them in reserve, for example at a point when the customer tries to push down either the price or the time needed for delivery, or when he makes an attempt to get more for his money. You may be the only supplier with different alternatives to offer. If you present these to the customer too early, there is the risk that he will go another round with your competitors, giving them the chance to add to what they already offered based on the alternatives that you have presented or developed.

Giving the customer an offer that represents a rough estimate

There may not always be enough time for you to provide an offer that is thoroughly worked out. Doing so can also be too expensive. There may be many different ways of solving a customer's problems. The customer may need to analyze more thoroughly than he

has already what he needs. In cases such as these, you may decide
to present more of a sketch than a detailed solution. Simply offer a
rough estimate of the costs, delivery time and resources that would
be required. You can then use this rough estimate as a basis for
negotiations where the two of you can work together to find solutions that will result in added value, in which the resources required
bear a sensible relation to the value that your offer has for the customer.

Being paid for your offer

A preliminary study is a type of offer that you get paid for preparing.
Even if no preliminary study is needed, however, you may decide to
attempt getting paid for the time you invest in preparing an offer, especially for any benefits the customer may realize from know-how
presented in the contents of your offer. Your offer may indicate, for
example, that the investment he originally intended to make would
not be worthwhile. The efforts you have invested will result in an offer containing information that will benefit the customer by helping
him to avoid an undesirable investment. He may even use your offer
to apply for a grant, for making a decision regarding future invest-
ments, for hiring new people, or for making various other important
decisions. All of these are considerations that can make him willing
to pay for your offer.

If the work required in preparing an offer involves considerable
costs – such as for tests, prototypes, trips or the work of an engineer
– it is particularly important to seek compensation for it. This can also be a test to see how interested the customer really is in purchasing
from you, or in keeping matters with you open until a final decision
is made. You can test him by asking for payment. When and how he
should pay can be a matter for negotiation in much the same way as
payment for a preliminary study.

If you never dare to ask for payment, so that you can see how the
customer reacts, you may miss out on some of your options.

When to decide not to make an offer

There are many factors that can raise warning signs against making
an offer. Among these are the following:

- *You fail in efforts to get the customer to change what he is willing to accept*
  If the customer is unwilling or unable to change the solution he is looking for, and this is unacceptable to you, then it may be pointless to make an offer, since it can never result in a contract.

- *The deal is not one for which you can sensibly compete*
  You have to accept reality. If you realize that what you have to offer does not measure up to what your competitors can offer, it is best to not submit any offer at all.

- *The customer wants an offer simply for comparison purposes*
  Here the customer has no intention of buying from you. He only wants an offer to compare with another, so that he can push down the price his usual supplier is asking, or perhaps to satisfy some official requirement, such as having to document having taken in offers from at least three different suppliers.

- *You risk giving away your know-how*
  You see no possibility, if you submit an offer, of protecting yourself against your know-how being passed on to others.

- *A deal cannot be completed, either for legal or for practical reasons*
  This could be a situation where you are unlikely to be paid, where you would not be given a permit to sell or carry on operations in the country in question. The resources needed (such as electricity, trained personnel or pure water) would not be available, or the foreign customer in question would only be allowed to purchase from a domestic supplier.

Summary of Phase 2 for the seller

1. Making a minimum price offer.
- When price is all the customer cares about.
- If the customer does not grasp the potential for obtaining added value.
- If low price is mainly all you have to offer.
- In order to get your foot in the door.
- In order to prevent your know-how from being taken advantage of.

2. Hold off making an offer.

- When the letter of invitation is suited to your competitors but not to you.
- If you know that the customer is not looking for the right things to meet his needs.

3. Using a preliminary study as a basis for selling.

- When not enough is known about the matter in question.
- In order to get your foot in the door.

4. Making an offer completely in line with the letter of invitation.

- Whenever making a competitive offer for a public contract.
- If the customer has gone to great lengths to specify what he wants.

5. Giving the customer alternatives to choose between.

- When you are unable to discuss things with the customer beforehand.
- To prevent having to compete purely on the basis of price.

6. Giving the customer an offer that represents a rough estimate of things.

- When you are short of time or if a complete offer would be too expensive to prepare.

7. Asking to be paid for your offer.

- If preparing the offer is expensive.
- When you feel you need to test the customer's sincerity.

8. Deciding to not make an offer.

- So as to get the customer to reassess things.
- When you suspect that the customer simply wants an offer for comparison purposes.
- If the deal would not be worthwhile for you.
- If you risk giving away your know-how.
- If the deal would not work out anyhow.

Phase 3 – Preparing an offer and getting ready for negotiations

Assessing your own needs, goals and resources

What do you want to achieve and what do you need to achieve in the negotiations? What persons in your organization would the signing of a contract affect? People in the production, experts in various areas, and service personnel can all contribute to negotiations with their knowledge and experience.

How will the buyer react to the needs and goals you express? What can you offer him? If your offer is to be effective, it should take into account the buyer's needs and the situation he is faced with. The quality of the solution you suggest and its supposedly good points need to be seen in relation to what the customer has use for.

The final goal you are aiming at and the offer you started with can differ greatly. If the price you want is $1,000, what should your opening price be? Certainly not $1,000! You need to have a margin. Thus, you should demand a higher price than this at the start. How much higher it should be depends on various factors, such as the branch of business involved, cultural norms that apply, and how strong the competition is.

What is at the basis of the needs you are concerned with and the goals you are pursuing? Unconscious desires may hinder your efforts to behave rationally here. If your aim is to show the customer that you know more than he does, there is a real danger that things will develop into a battle of prestige, where the arguments you present bring you further and further away from signing a contract.

Also be careful not to let the internal politics of your own organization affect your potential for signing a good contract. This may sound odd, but consider being faced with an unimaginative head of finance who does not want to provide a customer with credit, or a bureaucratic product manager who does not wish to deviate from manufacturing a standard product. Guarding yourself against the danger of groups or individuals within your organization manipulating you or each other to satisfy special interests is part of your job.

In successful negotiations you do not always move straight ahead to your final goal. Part of the time, the only goal you will be actively pursuing as a seller may be simply to meet the customer and see how far the two of you come, making the best of the situation. At some given point, it may be the customer who has the initiative, while you simply listen or respond, with no goal of making any immediate deal. He may be concentrating on any number of subordinate goals, such as gaining information or meeting the right people.

You will often be faced with conflicts between opposing goals. Your choice here may be particularly difficult if it is between "the Devil and the deep blue sea." Regardless of how you reason things out and in spite of your priorities, deciding on the goal to pursue at this point can be difficult.

Example
You work as a consultant and it looks as though within a month or so there will be a period of several weeks when you will have no project at all to work on, unless something unexpected turns up. Orders have been slow all year. Suddenly, a customer appears, like a gift from Heaven. He wonders whether you could help with something on short notice. The time period when you were going to have nothing else to do suits him fine. You prepare an offer and the two of you meet to discuss things. You have asked for your normal fee of $18,750.

The customer starts off saying, "I've just met with your competitor X, who's asking $12,500. I have a tight budget, and this is all I can pay. Do you want the job or don't you?"

You know that this competitor of yours has a price that is usually about 25 percent higher than yours. That means he cannot possibly be asking as little as that.

On the other hand, if you do not get the job, you will have nothing else bringing in money. You could use the time for marketing yourself and your firm. That might reward you with new jobs in the long run, but you will be out of money during this certain period.

• What priorities should you set between short-term and long-term goals?
• What goal should you be ready to fall back on, i.e. at what point

should you regard a deal as being so uninteresting that you should just say "no" to it?
• What goals collide with each other and in what way?

Keeping track of the time

A negotiator who is pressed for time is likely to be a poor negotiator. As he finds time running out, he may begin to lower his goals. If you realize you are under time pressure, be careful to avoid letting the other party know of this.

But consider this: as with other matters that you deal with, time itself can be negotiated. Consider the following thoughts and questions:

• How can you make the best use of whatever time remains? When you find you are under time pressure, maintain a fast pace and avoid unnecessary delays, such as those due to difficulties you or the other party may have in making a decision. Try to agree on goals that both of you can accept, such as "Today let's try to reach an agreement on the time schedule, the requirements our product should meet, and who else should be in on the decisions we make."
• Investigate the other party's time schedule. If that party wants the project to begin in October, you can send up a test balloon by declaring that it would be difficult for you to start then. See if the other party reacts by saying, "Well then, let's start in November", or by saying, "That would create a real problem."
• Try to negotiate for more time.

Example
The other party phones you up saying, "You've really caused problems for us here in the workshop! Your installation crew was supposed to be here at 8:00 this morning and now it's 10:30. We'll have to begin installing things ourselves so we can get the machine in operation by tomorrow. If we're delayed any longer than that, we'll lose too much money. You'll of course have to pay for the work our installation people do. Are we agreed on that?"

You're taken completely by surprise. The other party demands that you agree on the spot to paying them for work performed by their installation crew. You need time to think, to find out what's happened, what they'd been promised earlier and where your installation people are at the moment.

You could respond by saying, "I'm not in my office at the moment. Can I phone you back in about five minutes?"

In this way, you've negotiated for a few minutes to work on the problem. You manage to reach your installation people and find out they were delayed by a traffic accident. They assure you that they can be at the customer's place within 15 minutes, and that they'll work overtime if necessary so as to get the machine ready by the next day.

You didn't allow yourself be steam-rolled into going along with the other party's sudden demand, and you've saved your company unnecessary costs.

Your own risks, losses and gains

How important to you are the negotiations at hand? Do you have to succeed or have you got other potential customers? To figure out how much you can come down in price before you start to lose, consider what your chances would be with some other customer. If you have no alternative at all, however, it is more difficult to judge where that point would be. Suppose you have offered your services to a construction company for $75 an hour, knowing at the same time that you have a sure alternative working on a project for the city government at $62.50 an hour. You could consider $62.50 to be the lowest you will go when negotiating with the construction company.

Having desirable alternatives strengthens your negotiating position appreciably. It means you are not completely in the hands of the buyer. This prevents him from pressuring you into agreeing to a level that would be disastrous to you in the long run. It is only when you lack a viable alternative that you may feel forced into agreeing to something that is clearly to your disadvantage.

Since negotiations cost money and tie up resources, you should assess the cost of preparing an offer and conducting negotiations. Investigate the possibility of letting the other party bear some of the costs. Your biggest asset is your know-how. Figure out how you can prevent giving it away unnecessarily.

Keep in mind that the deal in question may fail to come off. What losses will you have then? What risks can you avoid, and how can you limit any damages the customer might try to collect? Your costs and your risks should bear a reasonable relation to your earnings and to the other advantages you can get. How large will these be?

Requirements the customer wants met

Is the list of requirements the customer provided you with complete? Are they actually requirements or is it simply a wish list? Do you have the required technical, economic and personnel resources? Is approval by some governmental authority necessary? If so, do you need to be certified in some way as a supplier and, if so, how?

Example
A firm in the telecommunication sector invested nearly a million dollars in preparing an offer. The expenses for developing and documenting the technical details required to meet the customer's needs were very high. Unfortunately, an important point was overlooked during the preparations: authorities in the customer's home country placed certain stringent requirements on suppliers. A supplier's production facilities had to be located in the customer's home country. No exceptions were allowed.

Not only had the company wasted a huge sum of money on a project that was doomed from the start, but it had also tied up its development resources and been forced to give up other opportunities. Nothing was wrong technically with the solution they developed. In fact, parts of it ended up being adopted by the company that got the job.

Legal aspects

Business activities are regulated by law. Which laws apply to the case in question? What do you have to do to comply with them? Do not forget laws on safety and protection of the environment. If business arrangements do not work out according to contract and a dispute arises, which laws apply then? If you are uncertain about such matters, be sure to consult with a lawyer before signing a contract.

To win a case in court, you have to be able to document that you are operating within the law. Make a habit of confirming everything in writing that has been agreed upon, any exceptions that have since been made, and your having adhered to whatever kind of formalities are involved. Even if your contacts with the customer appear to be positive in every respect, you never know what the future may hold. If things do not work out, both the buyer and the seller will be forced to take a careful look at what happened. How they view the situation here always tends to differ somewhat.

Example
For the last five years a supplier has sold his products to a customer in the public sector. The customer has always seemed perfectly satisfied. When the supplier mentions wanting to submit an offer for supplying what the customer will need for the coming year, he is told that the letter of invitation is not yet finished. The supplier brings the matter up again several times, but is repeatedly told that the letter of invitation has not yet been prepared. There is also no written documentation of the contacts made regarding this matter. However, the supplier might be viewed as being overly bureaucratic if each time they met he sent the customer a statement, such as the following: "In summarizing our discussion today, I note that I requested a letter of invitation for supplying you next year with the products we've supplied you with in the past. You informed me that the documents have not yet been prepared. I'll contact you again regarding this matter within the next 14 days."

When the supplier finally contacts the customer for what seems the umpteenth time, he is told that the order has already been given to a competitor. Thus, he had been given no chance at all to submit an offer. The customer has violated laws stating that a supplier who so requests has the right to receive a letter of invitation, one to which the same conditions apply as those given to any other suppliers.

Accordingly, the supplier has the right to claim damages for loss of earnings due to not having been given the opportunity to compete for the order. However, it is the supplier's word against the customer's. The customer declares that the supplier never asked to be given a letter of invitation and that a customer has no obligation to ask a previous supplier whether they want to compete for an order.

The supplier is forced to accept facts as they are. If he wants to be compensated for what he has lost, he will have to go to court.

Cultural considerations

Just as both the offer and the product should be adapted to what the customer needs, the approach you take with the customer should be adapted to his culture. This is just as true of contacts with customers inside your own country as with those outside.

There are cultural differences, for example, between men and women, between large cities and small towns, between technicians and economists, and between the public and private sector. Many companies have their own individual culture as well. It is important to be sensitive to cultural matters and adjust to them.

Example
During the Eighties, I helped IKEA (an international chain of furniture stores with its home office in Älmhult, Sweden) train its buyers. I'd agreed to this at a meeting in Stockholm with one of the training directors there. Just as I was about to travel to Älmhult for an initial meeting with some of their buyers, I phoned him to say my flight would leave Stockholm at 8:00 A.M.. He answered, "Good! Then I know when you'll be here."
When I arrived at his office, he remarked, somewhat incredulously,

> "You're here too early. You weren't supposed to arrive for another half hour."
> "We agreed that I was to take a flight from Stockholm at 8:00."
> "We did, but you can't be here this early."
> "But I am."
> "You can't be if your flight was at 8:00."
> "This makes no sense. If I'm here, then I'm here."
> "The bus from Växjö doesn't arrive for another hour."
> "Bus? I hired a car."
> "Who's supposed to pay for that?"
> "You are."

A cultural collision had occurred. Despite my having heard many times that IKEA's policy was to *use public transportation*, I had forgotten to conform to this. That I was also wearing a sport jacket and tie did not help matters either, since both of were taboo within the organization. Although I completed what I was supposed to do at the meeting, the chemistry of the situation did not develop as it should have.

Learning from your experience with previous negotiations

You have had experience with buyers of different sorts, but how well structured and easily accessible are your observations regarding them? It should be a requirement for sellers to maintain records of all negotiations in which he has been involved. From such records you should be able to see how different buyers behave and react, and what personal characteristics they possess. An example of records of this sort is presented in the section on negotiations as seen from the standpoint of the buyer, see page 23.

Take into account any changes that occur. Naturally, you will keep track of any effects caused by changes in technology, costs, market developments and the competition. But new people in key positions also represent a decided risk. Their backgrounds and loyalties are likely to be different from their predecessors. Some of them may show off by trying to turn everything upside down. Establish good personal contacts with them as early as you can.

What should your offer contain?

Usually, negotiations concern more than just one simple question (such as price, size of the order, or duration of the contract) but an entire package, the various parts of which are dependent upon each other. Any change in one part of the package can affect everything else.

Consider carefully how you will describe and present your offer. Should you include everything up front, or hold back certain things for tactical reasons? What would be the best timing for presenting your offer in order to help prevent competitors from getting wind of it?

How much leeway do you have in negotiating?

To be able to assess the different alternatives brought up in negotiations, you need to analyze factors that influence costs, profits and risks. These factors were discussed in some detail in the section on negotiations from the buyer's perspective, see page 33. The following discussion is an adapted version as seen from the seller's point of view.

Many such factors interact. Higher quality, for example, costs more but can provide the buyer added value in the form of lower maintenance costs, more reliable performance, higher residual value and greater protection of the environment.

For the decision making task to be manageable, you need to simplify it somehow by concentrating on those factors that have a direct and measurable effect on the result. What effects will these factors have on your total costs and profitability? To assess this, you need to translate the effect of these factors into the same measure, ideally monetary terms.

If you receive an advance payment, this gives you a gain towards loan interest. Some of what you gain here can be used to lower the price. Similarly, the customer may want you to shorten the delivery time. Doing this may make it possible for him to begin earning money sooner.

Even if you can shorten the delivery time without costing you anything, you should ask to be paid for this so you can profit from the added value the customer obtains. Two questions to always consider are in reference to how much it will cost you to make the concession the customer wants, and how much it is worth to him.

Identify factors that affect the overall result and compare the total costs and total gains involved in the different alternatives. Determine what you can negotiate, identifying factors you have a flexible view toward and are open to changing in some way. When you are sure about the areas that are open to change, ask yourself how far you are ready to go, or where you should set the limits. Consider the following example, which involves terms of payment, delivery time and a possible service contract:

Terms of payment: You could suggest a lower price against a 50 percent advance payment.
Delivery time: You could shorten the delivery time by as much as three months.
Service contract: You could agree to provide a service contract for up to five years.

Having thus determined the leeway you have for negotiating, or at least the extremes it would be sensible to agree to, the next issue will be to anticipate what the consequences will be of the various changes to the terms of agreement. Would they raise or lower the costs? Would they increase or lower earnings? Would they mean your risks being greater or less? Try if possible to express such consequences in monetary terms. The following is an example involving the factors just referred to:

Terms of payment: An advance payment would provide you a gain in terms of lesser interest on loan. An advance payment of 50 percent would be worth $19,000 to you.
Delivery time: Shortening the delivery time would cost you $12,500 for each month you shortened it.
Service contract: For a one-year service contract you would have to charge at least $25,000. For a contract of three years or longer, charging only $18,500 a year would be enough.

Advantages of having a negotiating scheme

Since most negotiations involve many different issues, you need to prepare yourself carefully. Attempt to get an overall view so you know where you are free to negotiate, how much leeway you have on various issues and what the positive consequences will be if you succeed in reaching agreement on any of the matters you are aiming at. It is important to keep track of things since this makes it easier to discover potential added value, and how to divide it up. It also helps you play an active role in discussions and to take the initiative. Having a negotiating scheme will be a big advantage.

Steps to preparing a negotiating scheme

The following steps can be suggested:

1. List all possible issues you think might come up, such as deadlines, price, performance, guarantees, payment schedules, hardware, software and questions of volume or numbers of items. Include not only issues dealt with in the offer, but others as well, such as the possibility of renting to the customer rather than selling to

him. Consider the residual value the product has, trade-in values the customer could get, service you could provide, installation, maintenance, and training of the customer's personnel.

2. Determine how much leeway you have in negotiations. In what ways might you increase or cut back what you are offering? This indicates how flexible you are when you negotiate and suggest alternative solutions.

3. Consider what the consequences would be for you if different changes were made. This will help bring to the surface issues that may be sensitive for you or have strong monetary consequences, as well as those that have little effect in monetary terms.

4. Try to get an idea of the leeway the customer has in negotiating different points. Does he have any alternatives that neither of you thought of?

5. Try to determine the effects different changes might have on the customer. Although it is difficult to form a complete picture, having as much information as possible makes it easier for you to discover matters you both can take advantage of.

Most of us have a less than perfect memory when it comes to the many facts and figures you should have at your disposal while negotiations are underway. A good negotiating scheme gives you the help you need here.

The following is an illustration of what a negotiating scheme might look like:

Variable	*Offer*	*Flexibility*	*Value*
Payment arrangements	100% upon delivery	We have use for 50% advance payment	This 50% has a value to us of $19,000.
Delivery arrangements	April 1, 1999	Jan. 1, 1999 at the earliest	Each month costs us $12,500.
Service	Not included in the offer	We can sign a service contract for 1-5 years.	A 1-2 year contract can be sold for $25,000 a year at the lowest, a 3-5 year contract for $18,500 a year at the lowest.

Conducting such an analysis will come in handy during later bargaining, enabling you to identify variables that can provide added value and deciding how to divide them up. Unless you know the variables involved, you risk giving the customer the initiative. The party that assumes the initiative has a better chance of taking advantage of the added value that has been gained. Remember, when deciding what you can best take advantage of in negotiations, take into account the customer's situation.

In the later discussion of the fourth phase for the seller, I will consider again how you can utilize information of the type that is summarized in the table above.

What opportunities does the customer have to negotiate?

Examine the negotiating scheme carefully, searching for variables the customer may have a flexible attitude toward. Attempt to determine how far he would be willing to go and what consequences a change in the terms of agreement would have for him. This will help you discover the added value that is available. Remember, added value comes about if a change in the terms of agreement is possible for both of you, and provided:

- your costs in taking over a task are lower than what it would be for the customer
- what the customer would gain is greater than it would cost you
- there would be gains for both of you.

Consider the following example:

Terms of payment: Interest costs are 13 percent for you and 14 percent for the customer. If you received an advanced payment, this would produce no added value at all, since what it would cost the customer is more than the amount you would save.

Delivery time: Each month earlier you can deliver than originally planned means an increase in earnings for the customer of $18,500, while costing you $12,500. You could shorten the delivery time by as much as three months. Doing so would produce an added value of $18,000 ($18,500 - $12,500 = $6,000 X 3).

Service contract: The customer wants to sign a service contract for two years, but not for any longer than this. He offers to pay you $30,250 a year for such a contract. If the lowest rate you would be willing to agree to is $25,000 a year, that would yield an added value of $10,500 ($30,250 - $25,000 = $5,250 X 2).

You have a problem, however, which is how to get your hands on this kind of important information. One way is to talk with people in the customer's organization. This is what we referred to earlier as back-door selling.

If you ask questions of these people, you may find yourself bar-gaining directly. Suppose you ask, "If we were able to deliver things to you earlier than requested, what would that be worth to you?" The conversation then might go as follows:

"How much earlier could you deliver it? I'll check whether there's an interest in this."
"We could deliver it three months earlier if what we got for this was enough to justify it."
"What would it cost you?"

Who is going to open up first and lay his cards on the table? What will you do if the customer is not willing to say how much an earlier delivery would be worth to him? If you answer his question by saying it would cost you "$12,500 a month," you will lose out on the added value that is there. The customer could say, "That sounds expensive. We could imagine paying you $8,750 to $10,000, but not more than that. Take another look at your figures."

If you bluff and say it would cost you $18,500 a month for each month, the customer would not make any profit and would probably say "no." The added value of $18,000 that could be gained would never be discovered or taken advantage of. How can such a problem be solved?

- You can avoid being greedy and can content yourself with asking for just $13,750 a month. This reduces the risk of your going fur-ther than the customer's strategy allows.
- You can avoid committing yourself and say that you would need around $13,750 to $15,000 a month.
- You can say you need to think it over.
- You can link this matter to various others to be negotiated. You

could say, for example, "If you accept the price we've offered you and sign a three-year service contract at $28,125 a year, we can shorten the delivery time by two months for $22,500." This even saves shortening the time by one month.

Analyze the customer's situation

You should have as thorough a knowledge as possible of those you negotiate with. Remember, negotiations are conducted not by organizations but by people. It is important to know, therefore, who you will be dealing with. What role within their organization does the person play? What authority has he been given? How are decisions within the organization made? What other people will be there?

Take into account anything special about the culture of the other organization. Try to put yourself in their place. What goals do they have? What do they need? What are their strong and weak points? You should know such things so as to be able to influence them as much as possible by your arguments and the line of reasoning you take. Such knowledge is no less important if you feel that the use of threats or a show of power is the best way to achieve your goals.

Example

Salespeople are often self-centered and want to show off about how much they know. Here is how an attempt on my part to buy the right car might turn out. Suppose I have two dogs, both of them St.Bernards. I want to buy a new car. For me, it is essential to have space enough for both dogs. I go to the local Volvo dealer to see whether he has a car with enough space. When I open the car's rear door and stand there wondering about this, a salesperson who makes the impression of being helpful arrives on the scene.

"I see that you're admiring our latest 850 model. Can I be of any help to you?"
"I'm wondering whether this car is large enough for me. I have two..."
The salesperson interrupts me:
"It's very large, as you can see. You have space for just about anything. Do you have a Volvo now?"

"No, I have an old SAAB."

"Then perhaps I could show you some of the finesses of the 850 that have made it the most popular large car on the road. You've probably heard that in the U.S. it's judged to be the most accident-safe car there is."

Why did he ask me whether I drove a Volvo? Is it because people who already drive a Volvo are to be treated in one way, while those who do not are to be showered with arguments as to why they should be driving a Volvo? The seller sounds like a parrot rattling off the arguments he has been taught. As he continues reeling off one argument after the other, I repeat my question about the size of the baggage compartment. He answers as follows:

"You'll be hard pressed to find a car that has more space. You can't imagine how much baggage fits in here. If you're planning to go on a skiing trip this winter, you should take advantage of the opportunity we're providing now to buy a roof-top luggage carrier. They are 50 percent off this week. If you fold back the rear seat, you have space there equal to a volume of 1,118 liters, as you can see here in our auto-graph."

When I hear "liters" and "auto-graph", whatever that is, I give up. For me, a liter is a bottle of milk. Translating St.Bernards into liters is more than I can manage. The meeting ends with my taking along a pile of brochures and hearing the salesperson spew his last few words.

"Phone whenever you like, and we'll set a time to look over your SAAB to see what your trade-in value will be. I'll see to it that you get top dollar for your old car. That's important when you trade in."

I have already decided, however, that I will not buy a Volvo, despite my knowing that it is a fine car, and still not knowing whether it would have space enough for the dogs. The salesman wore me out. In half drowning me with every different argument he had learned, he forgot completely to listen to what I had to say and find out what I was looking for. He showed no interest at all in knowing why I wanted a large luggage compartment. We never got off the ground in communicating with each other.

I continue my wanderings from one car dealer to another and end up at a place that sells Peugeots. My encounter with the salesman there starts off in the same way as it did at the Volvo dealer. I stand there examining the baggage compartment, when a salesman comes up.

"Can I help with anything?"
"Yes, I'm wondering whether the luggage compartment is big enough for me."
"It's large, as you can see. What do you want to put in it?"
"I have two large St.Bernards and I wonder whether they'd have adequate space in the back."
"That's hard to say. Where do you live?"
"Six miles from here."
"We can drive there and see if there's enough space for them. While we're doing that, you can try out the car."

While we're driving there, I have a chance to get to know the car. The salesman keeps a low profile and, instead of flooding me with information, he asks me a few things. Our conversation deals with matters I'm concerned about. When we get there, my dogs hop in. It turns out that they have plenty of space and they seem to like it there. I have no idea how many liters the baggage compartment would hold, but my dogs have enough space in it and that is what matters to me.

Try to imagine the many different surprises that can come up in negotiations. Preparing yourself will help considerably, but do keep in mind that no amount of preparation will ever cover all possibilities for what can happen. Reality tends to surprise you again and again. Your plan may not work out. The customer may set off in a completely different direction than you had expected. What do you do then? You should admit that you are involved in negotiations you are not prepared for. Realize that the signals you have gotten and the information you are now confronted with have changed your situation. Take a break. Analyze the situation carefully before you start off again. This involves not only working through your own checklist, but also attempting to go through the customer's checklist, which will help you see the negotiations from a different perspective.

Negotiations are based partly on facts and partly on expectations

You can be faced with a great deal of uncertainty when you negotiate. Always be prepared for the unexpected. Be conscious of the fact that your view of reality and of the negotiations you are involved in suffer from two serious limitations. One is that your perspective will naturally be very one-sided. The other is that your view is going to be incomplete. This calls for openness, careful attention to what is being said, and the ability to adjust to the situation. There may be much you will need to think through again before you are finished. Changes that suddenly occur can place you in a completely different situation than before.

It is dangerous to ever think you have found an approach you can continue with to the end. You do not know for sure what the other party will do. What should you do if he behaves completely differently than expected? There may be hundreds of different paths you could follow to get where you want. It is completely impossible to be fully prepared for all unexpected things that can occur. Remember, take a break when you need to reanalyze the situation and adjust to any facts or difficulties.

Nevertheless, you should be as well prepared as possible for a number of major alternatives. The approach I recommend is one I call *radial thinking*. Imagine you are a landlord and want to rent out a business space. The rent you want to get, figured on an annual basis, is $160 per square meter. Put yourself in the center of things and ask yourself for a moment how many different ways you might react if you were a tenant faced with the prospect of paying $160 per square meter rent.

As you can see in the first diagram (page 102), there are at least seven alternatives one could think of regarding actions or positions a potential tenant might take on the matter. What would you do as landlord if the tenant stated that the general level of rents in the area was only $100? As shown in the second diagram (page 103) there are five alternative actions the landlord might be expected to take. How would the tenant, in turn, react to any one of these?

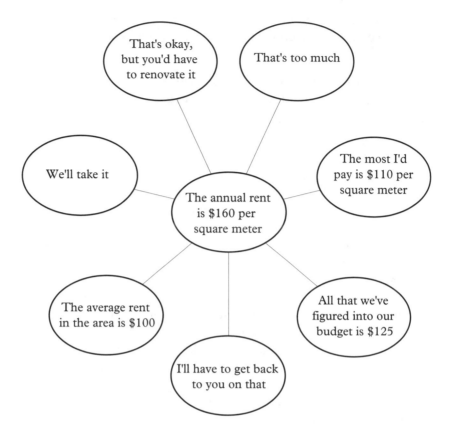

Prepare the arguments you will present

You should make a point of analyzing the strengths and weaknesses of your own position. Try to determine where your greatest strengths lie. Consider how you can utilize these most effectively. Concentrate on using only a few arguments, but strong ones. Aim at repeating them frequently and at translating them into benefits for the customer.

Example

If you simply argue, "We're the country's oldest and largest supplier of service of this sort," there's a strong risk that your argument will fall on deaf ears. The customer's reaction might be, "What good does that do us?"

If instead you say, "We're organized in such a way that we can

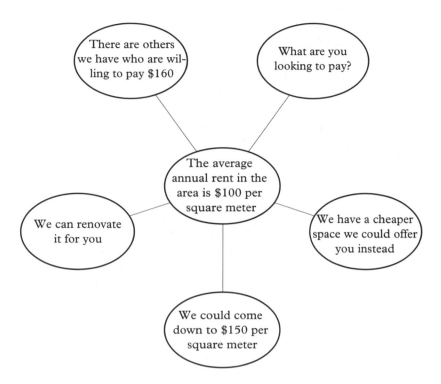

be at your door within four hours to begin resolving any problem," the customer understands much more readily the advantages of working with the oldest and largest company.

Do not forget to analyze your weaknesses too. If the customer knows about them, he can take advantage of them.

Example
While visiting your factory, the customer notes that production is not operating at full capacity. He is right in concluding that you have had too few orders come in, and that getting new ones is important to you. He can exploit this fact, trying to bring down the price. How should you deal with this when negotiations get underway?

1. Agree with the customer:
   "It's a good idea for you to purchase as much as possible now while the prices are low. If you place a larger order than you

usually do, we can give you a better price than what you're accustomed to paying."
2. Disagree with the customer:
   "Our orders are on the way up. We're planning to put in a new shift soon to keep pace with the demand."

There is no patent solution to a problem like this. Both ways of negotiating can be successful. Which of the two is best depends partly on the other party. The better you know the customer, the more freedom this gives you.

Some customers react positively to the first approach, understanding that you can help each other out. They are interested in keeping you as a supplier and are perfectly satisfied to get only a moderate reduction in price. Customers that react negatively see what you have said primarily as a confirmation of your desperation. They may decide to use power plays and threats in efforts to force down the price as much as possible.

The other approach represents kind of a game of poker. It can be successful with some customers who are not particularly tough on you, and also with customers who tend to always believe what you say. Others may see through your bluff, regard things as a matter of prestige, feel you tried to trick them, and do all they can to push the price down to a rock bottom level or, even worse, go to someone else.

Selecting members of your negotiating team and assigning roles

Who should be included on your negotiating team? Select these people and assign roles.

If the matters you are to take up are sufficiently important to economically justify bringing in available personnel, you should have a team of negotiators to help representing you. In selecting those who are to participate, you should assign each an appropriate role, just as I have pointed out in the previous section about negotiations as seen from the buyer's point of view, see p. 43.

The traditional division of roles between a chief negotiator, a technical expert, an economic advisor, and a lawyer, etc. is often not very satisfactory. The chief negotiator has a role somewhat analogous to that of an orchestra conductor. He takes the initiative in discussions, speaks for the group, makes decisions, and determines when other members should be brought into the discussion. He should assign the following supportive roles to other members of the group:

- *A listener,* whose main task is to listen to what is being said, observe what is going on and take detailed notes. During pauses in the proceedings, this person should be able to summarize for the others what has happened, what openings have appeared, how he feels the buyer has reacted, what signals he feels the buyer is trying to convey, and to what extent negotiations are proceeding as planned.
- *An evaluator,* who quickly digests new information that comes up and analyzes what it means, how it can be utilized, what economic implications it has and what solutions to the problem it suggests. This person is basically a navigator.
- *An alternative discussion leader,* who can take over as discussion leader when the need arises, giving the chief negotiator time to think, to digest information, or simply focus on listening to and observing the buyer.

Each of these people can have a double or multiple role, such as being an expert in one or more of the areas involved. However, it is the chief negotiator who calls upon each of the others in whatever role is required when the need arises.

Members should also agree in advance on how to communicate with each other. They should know how to warn the others if they realize that the chief negotiator is having difficulties, that he has missed a signal or that he is headed for a trap.

Always have a goal when you negotiate

As I have already repeated numerous times, be sure to always have a goal when you negotiate. Do not simply go to the negotiating table with a vague goal of making the best of the situation. If it is the other party that has asked you to come, find out what he wants and what his goals are. Think through and identify your primary goal, as well as any alternative or subordinate goals you may have.

These goals form the basis of the offer you present. To achieve a particular goal, you need to usually ask for more than what you hope to get.

Example

You are hoping to get a job at a particular company. What you are selling is yourself. At the moment, your monthly salary is $3,750. What should you aim for initially?

Unless you start off at a higher level than you are aiming for, you will never reach the goal you have in mind. If you sell yourself too short, no one will be interested in you. You decide to open at $4,000.

If you do not succeed in getting as much as $3,750, how much lower are you prepared to go? Can you imagine changing jobs without getting a higher salary? Suppose you say "yes" and decide the lowest you will go is $3,100.

Here is where subordinate goals come in. If you cannot get them to agree to at least $3,750, you can see whether it can be arranged for your salary level to be reevaluated after six months, after you have had a chance to show what you can do. You can also ask whether the employer would be willing to send you to a two-week training session that would make you better qualified for certain tasks.

Having an agenda helps you take the initiative

Consider having an agenda. You could prepare one, send it to the customer and suggest that the two of you follow it. This helps him to be prepared with answers to certain important questions, to be in a position to make decisions, and to ensure that the right people are available. As mentioned before, if your aim at the moment is not to discuss things with the customer in an easygoing way but to knock him off balance, you can introduce a surprise agenda. Again, to avoid being faced with such a situation yourself, and be able to prepare yourself by finding out what the customer plans to do, you can ask him to recommend an agenda for the meeting and send it to you.

Your agenda can also be completely internal, without the customer having any knowledge of it. This helps you prepare and provides you with an idea of what you should be aiming at.

Summary of Phase 3 for the seller

1. *Assessing your own needs, goals and resources.*
*   Have ready the offer you plan to open with, the offer you have as a goal, and any offers you are ready to fall back on.
*   Beware of conflicts of interest.

2. *Keep track of the time.*
*   Being under time pressure weakens your position and increases your risk of needing to make concessions to the other party.
*   Can you negotiate for more time?

3. *Your own risks, losses and gains.*
*   How important are the negotiations to you? What do you stand to gain?
*   What other customers do you have as alternatives?
*   What costs and risks do the negotiations involve?

4. *Requirements that need to be met*
*   Is the customer's list of requirements complete?
*   Does anything need to be approved by a government agency?

5. *Legal regulations.*
*   What happens if things do not work out and a dispute arises?

6. *Cultural considerations.*

7. *Learn from previous negotiations*
*   Keep records.

8. *What should your offer contain?*

9. *How much leeway do you have in negotiating?*
*   Prepare a negotiating scheme

10. *What opportunities does the customer have to negotiate?*
*   Can you make concessions and get something in return?

11. *Analyze the customer's situation.*
- Who will be involved in negotiations, what authority do they have, and how are decisions in their organization made?
- Cultural characteristics.

12. *Steps involved in preparing a negotiating scheme.*
- Issues involved.
- What leeway you have in negotiating.
- What consequences would various changes have?

13. *Negotiations are based partly on facts and partly on expectations.*
- Radial thinking.

14. *Preparing your arguments.*
- Concentrate on presenting a few strong arguments and repeating them frequently.
- Translate the arguments into advantages for the customer.
- What weaknesses do you have that the customer can take advantage of?

15. *Think things through before you negotiate.*
- Who will be on your negotiating team? What roles should its members have? Who should be the leader?
- How should you communicate within the group?
- Major goal?
- Agenda?

Phase 4 – Strategy

Establish a platform for bargaining and for reaching an agreement

Once negotiations begin, you should have some definite point of attack to get the ball rolling. You could ask the customer, for example, how the problem in question is being solved at the moment; and how this will affect their costs, earnings, risks and their situation in general. Also ask why they are doing things as they are. Starting off like this is often necessary if you are the one who has taken the initiative and the customer has yet to show any interest in having you submit an offer. You need to convince him that you have something better than what he has now. You want him to send you a letter of invitation to give you the opportunity of submitting an offer.

If the customer already knows what he wants and if he contacted you, the initial basis for negotiating will either be his letter of invitation or the offer you may have already submitted.

Before you get very far, you should ensure that the two of you are in agreement regarding how the letter of invitation and the offer are to be interpreted. Keep in mind how easy it is for one to misunderstand the other.

Determine what the customer needs and wants

Try to find out how the customer reacted to your offer. Do not be satisfied with him simply telling you, "That's too expensive." "That's not what we were looking for." "We've gotten a better suggestion from elsewhere." "We're shelving the matter for the moment." or whatever.

You need more information than that:

• What does the customer demand or expect of you? If he is not ready to accept your offer, find out what he wants. Get him to say what he needs in order to sign a contract.

- Which aspects of your offer does he want you to change? Why? What is he looking for? What needs or problems of his are at the basis of the demands or requirements he is expressing?
- What does he like about the offer you have submitted?
- What other alternatives does he have?

Example

Suppose your offer includes the following:

Delivery, installation and startup of the machine: $375,000
Terms of payment: 30 days net
Time of delivery: March 15th

"What do you think of our offer?"
"The price is too high."
"Too high? How do you mean?"
"It's higher than what your competitors are offering."
"What do you consider then to be an appropriate price?"
"If you went down by ten percent, your offer would be attractive."
"Are we agreed on things, apart from that?"
"No, we're not."
"What else are you thinking of?"
"We'd need to have it delivered earlier."
"When?"
"By February 1st."
"How is it with competitors of ours? When would they be able to deliver?"
"Earlier than you."
"As early as February 1st?"
"No, but earlier than the date you gave us."
"Okay. Is there anything else you're concerned about?"
"No, that's all we had in mind."
"Now I know what you want. What do you consider that we're particularly good at?"
"We've noticed that your products seem to have a high level of quality."

Get the customer to commit himself

Once you have received satisfactory answers from the customer regarding how he views your offer and the requirements that would need to be fulfilled for an agreement to be reached, it is time to get him to commit himself. You might say,

"If we can present you with a new offer that satisfies the requirements you've mentioned, a price that's ten percent lower than now and delivery by February 1st, could we agree to a contract on the spot?"

Note that this does not necessarily mean that you will end up accommodating the customer by reducing the price to the extent asked for. The point is simply to get the customer to make a statement of commitment and to prevent him from being able to play games with you and open up negotiations again at some later time on matters you have already agreed to.

If there is nothing specific that has been agreed upon and the customer has not committed himself to anything, negotiations can continue round for round until you are like a chicken that has been plucked. Regardless of what you offer the customer then, he will find fault with it and pit you against your competitors in a kind of auctioning procedure, where one supplier after the other is tempted to outbid the others.

The only answer of his you can regard as acceptable is, "Yes."

If the customer answers, "No," you need to find out why, where the problem lies and how it can be solved. Beware of indefinite answers such as, "We'll have to see about that. If the offer you end up giving us is a good one, then the contract is probably one we could sign."

Be alert to what is involved if you find the customer reluctant to close a deal. Try to find out if something is preventing him from signing. If he says he is waiting for an offer from a competitor of yours, hold off starting any serious bargaining. Try to arrange for a meeting again at a time when he is free to make a decision. If your next meeting takes place any earlier than this, you risk getting involved in an auctioning procedure in which, at each turn, the customer can say, "A competitor of yours gave us a better offer. Can't you improve your offer somehow?" Remember that your offer could also be seized upon by a competitor.

Reformulating the customer's demand for a lower price

A customer who demands that you lower your price is trying to get a better deal. There are other ways you can improve your offer, however, than by simply dropping the price.

Avoid all one-sided concessions. These reduce your profits and change the balance of power in favor of the buyer. Experience has shown that anyone who makes a one-sided concession easily goes on like this until he has given away everything. If you make a one-sided concession, it may be interpreted that your margin is so large you can afford to give things away. It also indicates that you are uncertain about your competitive position and the price you can get.

How can you provide the customer with economic advantages without simply making a one-sided reduction in price? One way is to reduce the price while at the same time demanding something in return: "If you give us an advance payment of 30 percent, we'll give you a five percent rebate. If you buy our standard machine instead of the advanced version, we can reduce the price by 15 percent. If you install the machine yourselves, we'll reduce the price by another $31,250." This allows you to retain your profit or even increase it, and maintain your negotiating strength as well. You also signal to the customer that when you give something up, you want something in return.

You can also raise the price, but in so doing give the customer more for his money. "I have another suggestion that might interest you. If you pay $18,750 more, you could have a machine with considerably greater capacity. It produces 125 units an hour, instead of 100."

Again, you will have kept your profit, or even increased it, and you are as strong in your negotiating position as before. The signal you give the customer here is that you are glad to help, but that you will do so in a different way than the customer had suggested. Reformulate the customer's demand to lower your price, while getting him to consider his overall economic advantages. If at all possible, help him from being blinded by the question of price.

Let us return now to the machine you offered the customer for $375,000 and to the customer declaring that this was too expensive, demanding that you lower your price by at least ten percent.

Example

"You said for there to be a deal we'd have to cut ten percent off the $375,000.

"That's right."

"Then we'll need to make you a new offer that will result in a $37,500 improvement in where you stand economically."

"What do you mean?"

"I mean that we cannot simply lower the price, but we can try to find a solution that will put you $37,500 ahead, compared with the offer we gave you originally."

"If it actually does put us $37,500 ahead, then it might work."

"If we find a solution that will do just that, do we have a deal?"

"Yes, assuming that it actually is worth this much to us."

Looking for solutions that provide added value

Added value can potentially be achieved under any of the following conditions:

- If redistributing work and responsibility between you and the other party would lead to a reduction in the project's costs. In the case above, the $375,000 the customer was to pay for the machine included installation. Suppose you figure that your costs for installation would be $37,500, whereas the customer would be able to do it for less than this, say for only $21,000. Letting the customer take over the work and responsibility of installing the machine would thus reduce the costs by $16,500 ($37,500 - $21,000). (For this to represent added value for the customer, it would be essential, of course, for him to have the personnel, technical facilities and know-how for performing the installation).
- If changes in the terms of payment would reduce the project's costs. Suppose the 30 days terms of payment were changed, allowing you to get 40 percent of the amount as an advanced payment. This would save you interest, but would create interest costs for the customer. If you saved $25,000 in interest, while the increase in interest costs to the customer was only $17,500, an added value of $7,500 would be created ($25,000 - $17,500).
- If the customer would profit from earlier delivery. Suppose the customer's letter of invitation included a request for delivery by

March 15th. Further suppose that you incorporated this date into your offer, but that the customer then discovered he could really benefit from having the machine by February 1st. Now assume that this six-week gain in time would be worth $37,500 to the customer, because it would allow production to start earlier than originally thought necessary. The extra costs to you for making this possible would be only $6,250. This would result in an added value of $31,250 ($37,500 - $6,250).

Examine carefully each of the variables your offer contains, asking yourself whether any of these might present a solution, resulting in added value. The customer might be interested in trading in an old machine for a new one, for example, or you could see whether he would need training for personnel in use of the machine and whether he might want a service contract.

If the customer shows no interest in opportunities of this sort, do not simply leave it at that. Try to find out why and whether anything could be done to change this.

Example
You find the customer does not want to install the machine himself. Try to determine why:

"We don't want to take on any responsibility for delivery or installation of the machine," the customer declares, "because if any problems arise later, we might disagree on whether this was the fault of the machine or how it was installed."
"Yes, I understand, and we can provide someone who'll take charge of the installation. So, presuming you would agree that this person will have complete responsibility and authority for making sure that things are done properly, and if you supply us with three electricians to do the job, then we will assume responsibility for ensuring the machine functions properly."
"We could consider a solution of that sort."

Gaining insight into the basis for the buyer's calculations

Gaining insight into the basis for the buyer's calculations is one of the most difficult yet critical tasks required in bargaining. Suppose the buyer says he would be willing to make an advance payment of 40 percent. How can you find out what this would cost him? Take the initiative and ask directly: "What would it cost you to make such a payment?" If you fail to take the initiative, the buyer can take the initiative by asking, "If you get an advance payment of 40 percent, how much would you be ready to come down in price?"

What difference does it make whether it is you or the customer who asks first? If the customer asks first and you answer that it would be worth $25,000, the customer is likely to ask for a reduction by that amount, even though his costs might be considerably less. If you ask first and the customer answers, saying that an advance payment would cost him $17,500, then you have the opportunity to keep all or part of the added value of $7,500.

If the customer wants a shorter delivery time, what can you ask for in return?

Example

"We can always invest in extra help or work overtime to get the machine finished for you earlier," you say, "but how much could this be allowed to cost for it to still be worthwhile for you?"

"Well, do you know how much higher your costs would be?"

"I'd have to do some figuring, but do you know how much it would be worth to you?"

"It's hard to say, but if you could get your calculations done and get back to us, we can judge whether it would be worthwhile."

Here, neither you nor the other part wants put his cards on the table. You both appear to agree that there would be costs involved in shortening the time, but whether there is added value to be had, and if so, how this should be divided up between you is something you have to be able to talk about.

"I've done some figuring. The preliminary figures I've arrived at suggest that the extra costs of an earlier delivery like this would be about $12,500."

"That sounds pretty high. If it had cost somewhere in the area of $6,250, that would have sounded all right."

"That's not possible, but we might be able to come down to between about $10,000 and $11,250."
"Or down to $9,250?"
"Well, I'll have to get back to you on that. Let's say that if we shorten the delivery time by six weeks it would be worth at least $9,250 to you."

You should not agree to anything before you have discussed all the variables involved and tried to squeeze as much information as possible out of the other party. At the end of each discussion, summarize what the two of you have arrived at: "Let's note that if we shortened the delivery time by six weeks it would be worth a minimum of $9,250 to you."

Before presenting a new offer, summarize what has been said, take a break and analyze the situation

Once all points have been covered, make a summary of where you are. Take a break and consider carefully what your new offer should be and how you should present it to the customer.

Example
"We've agreed that, for it to be a deal, the arrangement we made would have to put you $37,500 ahead, compared to how things were in our original offer."
"That's right."
"Then let's shake hands on that here and now."
"Right!"
"We take on the complete responsibility for the installation being done properly and we provide the person who will be in charge. You, in turn, supply us with three electricians to do the job. You will be reimbursed for the work they do, being credited $15,000. Is that how you've understood things?"
"Yes, that's right. That's the way we've understood it."
"Regarding the terms of payment, you will give us an advanced payment of 40 percent, for which you will get a $17,500 rebate."
"That's correct."
"And then there's the matter of the delivery time, where we said we'd do what we can to shorten it. If I've understood you

correctly, it would be worth at least $9,250 to you if we made delivery by February 1st."
"That's correct too."

You can now calculate the price the customer would be paying in terms of the offer just described:

Basic price	
(of $375,000, reduced by $37,500 or 10 percent)	$ 337,500
Deduction for the customer's installation costs	
(three electricians)	-$ 15,000
Deduction for the customer's cost in making an	
advanced payment	-$ 17,500
Adding in what the customer gains through	
delivery by February 1st	+$ 9,250
Final price (new)	$ 314,250

Presenting the customer this new price, you can show him that you have taken into account everything agreed upon. You have figured in the costs and the gains the customer declared he had in connection with the different parts of the overall package. You had also gotten the customer to commit himself by his agreeing that it would be a deal if his position could be improved by at least $37,500.

You then take a look at how you are affected by the package that has been agreed upon.

Reduction in price		
($375,000 - $314,250: see list above)	-$	60,750
Saved through the customer installing the machine	+$	37,500
Value of receiving an advanced payment	+$	25,000
Costs of delivery by February 1st	- $	6,250
Your net costs	- $	4,500

So, to be able to offer the customer the $314,250 price referred to above, you have to take $4,500 out of your own pocket. This is decidedly better than losing the entire $37,500 by which the new offer was to be improved, and which the two of you agreed upon.

Submitting a new offer

Before submitting the new offer you have worked out, you should think about the following:

- *How can you avoid a situation where the customer begins a new round of negotiations with the other suppliers?*
  This can be avoided by getting him to commit himself, confirming that he will sign a contract if his demands are met.

- *Do you need to satisfy all the demands the customer has made?*
  It may be necessary only to address some of them. It may not even be necessary, for example, to drop the price by the full $37,500. On the other hand, the faster delivery time you want to provide may be worth more than $9,250 to him. If you think there may still be room to negotiate some point, you should make a counter-offer that allows you to test how far the customer is willing to go. You might offer $343,750, for example, for the new package. If the customer accepts, this gives you an additional profit of $25,000 ($314,250 + $4,500 = $318,750 + $25,000 = $343,750).

- *Should you signal your readiness to compromise when you make your counter-offer?*
  What you could say is, "At a price of $343,750, you should be able to get back what you invested." Realize the dangers involved in being high-handed, avoiding statements such as, "Take it or leave it!"

- *What should you do if the customer fails to accept your offer despite meeting his demands?*
  Try making a counter-offer. Test again how far he is willing to go. Remember that whenever you accommodate him, you should always ask for something in return. Consider the possibility of giving him more rather than reducing the price.

What if the customer does not accept how you want negotiations to be conducted?

In looking at the strategy the customer's checklist involves, you may anticipate difficulties in steering negotiations in a direction you would prefer. Each of you may end up trying to take the initiative.

If the customer fails to clarify what he is aiming at and makes things generally difficult for you, you may be forced to change your strategy. Think about the following:

- Never make one-sided concessions.
- Offer the customer alternatives.
- Do not give up. Try later on in negotiations to make a counter-offer that allows you to get the customer to commit himself, and in such a way that ensures you will not be forced below the minimum level that you want to adhere to.
- Realize that it is better to drop things altogether than to end up with a deal that is to your disadvantage.

Record your negotiations

Again, remember that although oral agreements are binding, be sure to get everything in writing. Written documentation is the best way to ensure adherence to any agreement. And remember, if you formulate the contract, it will be the customer who is obligated to contact you if he has a different conception of what has been agreed to.

Document, summarize and analyze everything that has taken place during negotiations. This will better enable you to use the experience you have acquired. Follow up on things and contact the customer as soon as you discover or suspect that something should be changed or renegotiated, or when something has gone wrong.

Summary of Phase 4 for the seller

1. *Establish a platform for bargaining.*
- Use the customer's present situation, his letter of invitation or your offer as a starting point.

2. *Find out what the customer needs or wants.*

3. *Get the customer to commit himself.*

4. *Reformulate the customer's demand for the price to be reduced.*

5. *Look for solutions that create added value.*

6. *Gain insight into the calculations the buyer has made.*

7. *Summarize what happened during negotiations.*
•   Take a break.
•   Look for added value and considering how it can be divided up.

8. *Submit a new offer.*

9. *Consider what to do if the customer does not go along with how you want negotiations conducted*

10. *Record the negotiations.*

Advice on how to negotiate

Advice for negotiators

In this final section general advice is provided on the subject of bargaining. Always keep in mind that this is a process of give and take. Many people are not good at this. They have a strong resistance to the idea of bargaining and feel it is beneath their dignity. Most readers have probably spent little time, if any, bargaining with merchants in a bazaar. However, if you have no mastery of the art of bargaining, this will greatly limit your ability to behave in a businesslike and cost-effective manner when negotiating.

In addition, I want to consider the topic of communication. Unless communication functions properly, negotiations will never become truly constructive. Poor communication, such as when neither party is able to get through to the other, frequently causes negotiations to flounder. I will take up various ways in which communication can fail and how certain pitfalls in communication can be avoided. I will also point out how everything in negotiations is relative, even supposed positions of strength. A person who feels his negotiating position is so strong that this alone will suffice to achieve what he wants can suddenly be forced into the realization that this view was not consistent with reality.

Finally, I want to emphasize the importance of good personal relations in negotiating successfully. A deal being made between two persons is often based to a very high degree on how they interact, on the chemistry of it all. The matters discussed, such as questions of finance, quality or performance, can often be dealt with rather easily if the two are on the same wavelength.

Bargaining

Bargaining is a central aspect of negotiating. It involves two parties dividing up costs, risks, responsibilities and profits by making offers and counter-offers, and by making concessions while getting something in return. In many parts of the world people seem to regard price as entirely fixed. With few exceptions, such as the buying and selling of cars, where bargaining is accepted, many people seem to want prices for everything to be clearly stated from the beginning. However, in the world of business negotiations, nothing is ever set in stone. To succeed in business, ensuring profitability and avoiding unnecessary risk, you must be able to bargain effectively.

Example
Let's look at a meeting between a buyer and a seller. The buyer opens by saying,

> "There's one point in your offer I'd like you to adjust. We want 90 days credit. You've only offered 30."
> "Thirty days is the longest period we can offer."
> "Then there's no way we can accept your offer. We can't go along with a deal of any sort unless we can get 90 days credit."
> "I'm simply not authorized to give you a longer period than that. In every country where we do business, 30 days is the most we give."
> "Phone the home office to be sure. Check with them."
> "There's no point. Our administrative routines are based on giving 10, 20 or 30 days credit. What I've offered you is the best we have."
> "If that's the case, we'll have to forget about it. We're not interested."
> "I might be able somehow to get you a 45-day credit. But that's really the best and last offer we can make. None of our other customers could possibly get a longer extension on payment than that."

"Why are you offering us only 45 days when what we want is 90?"

"Each of us has to make some sort of concession."

"What are you suggesting, that we make a compromise?"

"Yes, I am."

"What you suggested before was a bit on the stingy side. It's not a fair compromise if we're supposed to give up 45 days and you're only willing to give us 15. If you'd said 60 days, then each of us would have gone halfway. Give us 60 days, and we'll have a deal."

Bargaining of this sort is characterized by both parties first arguing for their standpoint, trying to get the other party to give in, using arguments that are often false or one-sided, with neither party being influenced by what the other is saying. Such negotiations are like a game of poker. If neither party gives up, one of them usually threatens to do something, forcing the other party to either abandon what he is arguing for or test whether the threat is for real. The solution that is reached often lies about halfway between what the two parties were claiming they should get. Neither party wants to lose out or to back down more than the other.

In attempting to be clever and influence the other party, people who negotiate in this manner use arguments that are partly false. People can easily lose confidence in them. In the example here, the seller says first that he is not authorized to give credit for a longer period of time. Confronted with the threat of losing the sale, he backs down and offers 45 days credit. Then he says it is his final offer, but moments later offers 60 days credit. The buyer accepts, despite having declared a few moments earlier that there would be no deal if he did not get 90 days. A negotiator who bluffs in this way loses whatever confidence people might otherwise place in him.

Was it a good solution the two parties ended up with? The seller was forced to give the other party another month's credit, which was a monetary loss. What did he get in return? Nothing! All that the customer gave up was an exaggerated demand for 90 days credit. A compromise of this sort is one-sided, since there is really only one party that gives anything. Suppose the customer actually did need 90-days credit. Was this need then satisfied? No. He would still be hard-pressed for cash when bills came due. When the two parties finally agreed to 60 days credit, it was perfectly clear to each of them that the other party had been lying. Thus, any continued negotiations would tend to be characterized by mutual distrust.

If we asked the seller why he gave in, he might answer, "I'm better off accepting the costs of giving credit for a longer period than ending up without a sale. Even though this costs me $10,625 more, I'm still within my margin of $15,000, so I can afford it." If we asked the customer why he had tried so hard to get a longer credit on payment, he might answer, "We save a lot of money by managing to get extended periods of credit on what we buy. The extension we got in this case gave us $7,500."

They arrived at a solution that cost the seller $10,625 but was worth only $7,500 to the customer. What happened to the difference between these two sums, which amounts to $3,125? That sum is the price the negotiators paid for using the wrong approach in negotiating with each other.

Their mistake was to know nothing of what a change in contract terms meant for the other party. If we had said to the buyer that he should find out what it would cost the seller to extend an extra month credit on payment, he might have answered, "I don't care what it costs him as long as I get what I want." If the customer had asked the seller what it cost him, the answer would have been $10,625. If the customer had then reflected on this, it would have been clear to him that the seller's interest costs for a one-month period were higher than his. Thus, no added value was created by the seller providing the customer with a longer credit on payment. The costs were greater than the gains.

Suppose, instead, that the customer made use of this information and said, "Then we'll have to rethink the matter. In my estimation, it's better if we solve the problem of credit in some other way. If we go back to the 30 days credit in your original offer and stick with that, that'll allow you to avoid $10,625 extra in interest costs." The seller should be satisfied with this. Suppose the customer then continues by saying, "But if you can hang onto this $10,625, I want you to come down in price. Reduce the price by, let's say, $9,375."

What's the result of that compared to the seller providing a 60-day credit? The seller ends up saving $1,250 ($10,625 - $9,375) and the customer wins $1,875 ($9,375 - $7500). The customer could then suggest, "Let's go one step further. If I pay cash instead of getting a

30-day credit, you save an additional $10,625 in interest. I'd be willing to pay cash, but then you'd have to come down by another $9,375 in price. "

Conclusion: Beware of false compromises. Threats, bluffs and cutthroat competition can easily result in solutions where both parties lose. Note the consequences a particular change in the terms of contract would have for you and let the other party know about it. You may both end up then discovering added value that each of you can take advantage of.

Making concessions to the other party

Experience and research show that one party making concessions to the other is not only a normal part of bargaining, but is often a deciding factor in determining the net result of negotiations.

Ensuring that you have leeway to negotiate

Skill in being able to select the right level to start at is another important factor in achieving good bargaining results. Regardless of whether your role is that of a buyer or a seller, you should be sure that your initial position gives you leeway to negotiate. For a seller, this would involve asking a sufficiently high price to begin with, whereas a buyer would initially ask for a price that is low. However, it is not necessarily the price or other financial considerations that needs to be high or low in order for you to have sufficient leeway. First consider other demands you expect the other party to try to get you to reduce or drop. If such an approach is to be successful, you have to demand, for any change of this sort, that the other party gives you something in return.

This may sound simple enough, but it is much more difficult in practice. There are traps of two opposing kinds you can fall into.

Demanding too much initially

If your demands are too high at the start, the other party is likely to either not take you seriously or not be interested in doing business with you. At the same time, it is not easy to know where the other party will draw the line in this respect. There are also strong cultural differences, particularly between certain countries, regarding how far apart the buyer and the seller tend to be when negotiations begin. In some countries each party will have an initial margin of perhaps 2-20 percent. In far more extreme cases, an offer of 300 by the seller may be responded to by a counter-offer of 10, with the two of them finally agreeing on a price of say 25-30.

There are different ways to avoid the danger of demanding too much from the start. Before negotiations get underway, you can attempt to determine what price level the other party could agree to accept. If your role is that of a seller, you can make up a list for yourself of prices that seem reasonable to suggest for various alternatives. Be as well informed as possible regarding what value a particular offer would have for the buyer. In addition, you can attempt to optimize your timing, learning to not present an offer until the right moment appears.

You can also keep two prices in mind: that which you intend to begin with, and that which you are ready to come down to. In addition, you can use some of the strategies for making offers that I described in the chapter on Phase 2 from the standpoint of the seller.

Not being taken seriously if you give up your demands while demanding nothing in return

It has now been pointed out numerous times that if you simply give things away, you are not only hurting yourself and your company unnecessarily, but you quickly lose credibility. The other party will begin to assume that you always have a large margin and that, if he presses you hard enough, he can get you to reduce it. He may also feel uncertain regarding the level he should agree to, wondering whether the conditions you are offering could be vastly improved. The easiest way of avoiding this is to never give away anything without receiving something in return.

Getting the other party to reveal his wishes and demands

Get the other party to reveal what he is looking for and hoping to get. Find out what his needs are, which will help explain why he is making certain demands or expressing certain preferences. Hold back at the start regarding any arguments or views you may have on the matter. You need to have sufficient information before you can analyze properly what the other party appears to want. Once you feel you have grasped the other party's views regarding a possible contract, you can attempt to close the deal. Simply ask, "If we succeed in being able to provide you what you've made clear that you want, can we agree to signing a contract?"

If this essential matter is dealt with satisfactorily, you can take a break from what you are doing and examine the other party's demands carefully. Ask yourself what added values can be discovered, what opportunities there are to negotiate, which demands are easy to reject, and which of them should be met either fully or partway. You seldom need to meet all the demands the other party claims are essential for a contract to be signed.

Avoid making one-sided concessions

A party that begins negotiations by making one-sided concessions achieves less in the end. Such concessions tend to be interpreted as a sign of weakness, as a lack of ambition, or as your having such a wide margin in your favor that you can afford to be generous. This can lead to a chain reaction that ends up with your losing to the other party all or most of what you had. A one-sided concession should only be made under special circumstances, such as for closing a deal, or for getting negotiations started up again if they have come to a standstill.

Let the other party work hard for any concessions you give. If you make a concession at the start, this generally gets you nowhere, since at that point there is usually no decision to be made and the other party thinks only of what it can grab hold of. It is important for psychological reasons that you force the other party to fight for the concessions it gets. Otherwise, it loses out on the satisfaction of being able to attribute getting these concessions to its skill in negotiating. If you do things right here, both of you win and you also keep the other party in a good mood.

Example
You apply for a job at a firm. Your present salary is $2,750 a month. You would like to get at least $3,100. You realize that to get this latter amount you will have to ask for an even higher

amount. When the matter of salary is discussed, the person interviewing you asks,

> "What salary are you looking for?"
> "I feel I'm worth at least $3,300."
> "Did you say $3,300?"
> "Yes."
> "Then you're welcome to start working for us next week."

At least nine out of ten people hired in this way would be dissatisfied with this result, feeling they could have gotten more had they asked for it.

Looking at another example, if offered a longer guarantee period, a buyer might in return sign a service contract or agree to paying you a higher price. If the buyer rejects the suggestion, your position is in no way weakened. You are free to go on looking for some other opening that could likewise lead to mutual concessions being made.

When concessions are only made on your part, you strengthen the other party's position. This upsets the power relations between you. The other party can then exploit the advantages and force you to give away more than you have given away already.

An important point to make here is that, when looking for an opening that can lead to concessions from both sides, always state what you want the other party to concede *first*, *then* reveal what you are ready to give in return.

Example

> "We can come down five percent in price, but then you'd have to be ready to buy an additional 20 percent of your yearly requirements from us."
> "Let's see, if the price was five percent less, what would it be?
> "It would be $2.50 per unit."
> "Okay, I'll note then that you're offering it to us now for $2.50 a unit. If we could agree to also adjusting the terms of payment somewhat, that would seem reasonable. We'd like to have 30 days to pay."
> "Yes, but what do you say to the increase in the amount that you purchase?"

> "We'll have to get back to you regarding that. Are we agreed on the terms of payment?"
> "Yes."
> "Are you willing to ship it to us free of freight charges? Your competitors charge nothing for freight."

The seller has failed here to get the customer to commit himself. Thus, he has lost his grip. He showed his cards too early and was forced into making one concession after the other. A seller who was alert to pitfalls of this sort would have been more cautious:

> "If you could imagine buying an additional 20 percent of your yearly requirements from us, we could make an adjustment in the price."
> "What price would you give us then?"
> "Are we agreed that you'd buy 20 percent more from us than what you usually buy?"
> "That would depend on whether we got a good price."
> "Could we deliver this 20 percent to you during the first three months of the year?"
> "That would be okay, but what price would we get?"
> "Are we in agreement regarding everything else? Is price the only thing left?"
> "Yes."
> "What would you consider a good price?"
> "About $2.30 a unit."
> "We couldn't go that far, but we could come down 3-4 percent."

While you are preparing for negotiations, you should consider the different concessions you can ask the other party to make. When negotiations are underway and you have to deal with the different demands that can be placed on you, you will have little chance to analyze carefully which concessions by the other party would be appropriate.

Be careful to compute things properly

Be clear about the sums of money you will be taking in and paying out. Attempt to determine what your concessions would be worth to the other party. Note that a concession on your part that costs you nothing may be worth a lot to the other party. Anyone trying to get you to make concessions may present the amounts of money involved in such a way that you can easily fail to grasp what it would cost you.

Shortening the delivery time, for example, may not cost you anything, but it could allow the buyer to get production underway earlier than planned and increase his profits considerably. Each month of having the machine he bought from you for $1,250,000 in operation might put him $25,000 to $37,500 further ahead. In such situations both of you can benefit.

Example
During the final minutes of negotiations that have been going round and round for several months, the buyer who wants to lease 120 cars for a three-year period requests that the auto dealer install a stereo radio in cars whose drivers want it. He indicates that if this is agreed to, he will sign the contract. He tells the seller, "You make only $10.60 for such a stereo. If you agree to this, we'll sign." The seller spends a few seconds considering the matter and says, "Okay." He has not made any calculations of what it would cost. As it turns out, since having the stereo does not increase the price, all of the drivers want one and get it. The costs to the seller, however, are considerable. Multiplying the monthly rental fee of $10.60 for each stereo by 36 months, and this by the 120 cars, leads to a sum of $45,792. The multiplication involved is not something you can easily carry out in your head, at least not within a matter of seconds.

Say "no" if you mean "no"

I you do not want to go along with what the other party requests, clearly state, "No." Do not respond with any of the following:

Example
"I don't think we could manage that."
"I'm not authorized to agree to that."
"We'd have to think about it."

"We can't do much about the price."
"We've pretty much given all that we can."

If you answer in that way, the other party will succeed in getting what
he wants. He will take note of your uncertainty and exploit it. Learn
to say "No", and stick to it.

Stick to your final offer

Do not make concessions unnecessarily. If you can achieve what you
want elsewhere, you are better off leaving things as they are and making clear to the other party that the offer you have given is what a contract will involve. Leave the choice to him. Indicate that you have
treated him just as your other customers are treated and that you do
not haggle about prices or terms of contract. You can of course offer
one or more alternative solutions if you have any. Just be rigid and
unbending regarding the contractual terms you have arrived at, while
remaining flexible about how you present things.

A compromise does not mean you have to meet the other party halfway

If the other party suggests that you reach a compromise, such as by
sharing extra costs of $12,500, this does not necessarily mean that
each of you should go halfway, both paying $6,250. When the other
party suggests a compromise, this generally means that he has given
up and, in this case, that he is ready to pay *at least* $12,500 so as to
get the matter over and done with. He may even say, "Let's share
things 50/50." You should answer, "That's more than I can manage,
but perhaps I could pay 30 percent of it." You may discover, if you
immediately put your hand out to finalize the matter with a handshake, that in many cases the other party will accept a 70/30 arrangement, as long as this is an amount he is able to bear.

Research on making compromises in this way has shown that under such circumstances you can often interpret the other party's offer
as follows. If he suggests a compromise, his goal is usually that you
divide things up evenly. If you want to see how far he's willing to go,
you can divide things in half once more and suggest 25/75.

You may be asked, "Can't we compromise on this $12,500 so we can get that problem out of the way?" If you respond, "Okay, I can take half of it," he could respond by declaring "That's not enough. I can't take on more than a quarter of the total amount." It is a big and dangerous move, therefore, to unequivocally state that you are willing to carry half of the sum.

So as not to be the party that loses when things are divided up, you need to open cautiously: "Yes, I could probably take on 10-20 percent of it." Do not be in too much of a hurry when you bargain. Suppose you have offered a buyer a two percent rebate and have the option of going up as high as eight percent, but that the buyer feels two percent is too little and demands six percent for agreeing to a contract. In such a situation, many sellers are tempted to counter with four percent. That is a dangerous move! Anyone who raises an offer from two percent to four doubles his offer, and thus signals both naive generosity and having a large margin to negotiate with. If the customer is observant, he can go ahead and demand seven percent.

The seller can protest, "But what you asked for just now was only six percent!"

The customer could counter by saying, "No, I said at least six or seven percent."

If the seller, instead of making a counter-offer of four percent, had taken time to analyze the customer's demand for a six percent rebate, he could have concluded that the customer's goal was to achieve four percent, and to not go below three percent. In light of this, he could have presented a counter-offer of 2.6 percent. A seller who does this realizes the importance of taking only small steps. Going up to only 2.6 percent sends a completely different signal to the customer than going up from two percent to three or four.

Bear in mind the psychological and economic importance of advancing in steps of fractions of a percent, rather than whole percentage numbers. Even thousandths and ten-thousandths can be divided up into fractions of a unit.

Coming to an immediate agreement is not necessary

You do not need to take an immediate stand regarding a demand or wish the other party has. Taking a break can give you an opportunity to find other solutions. It also makes the other party uncertain as to whether he has gone too far.

If you do not know what to do, you can always try to bind the other party to the offer he has already made by asking him for an option on it. That means that you have the right but not the obligation to accept the offer, while he, on the other hand, is bound to this offer.

Say, "I can't give you an answer on that matter immediately, but I'd like to have an option on your offer. If I could have a chance to study it more carefully, I can get back to you in a few days with an answer. If we can accept your offer, then we'll have a deal."

You now have the option of accepting the offer, of accepting some parts and negotiating others, or of declining the whole thing.

Summary of bargaining

- Avoid false compromises.
- Investigate the effects of any possible changes in the terms you agree to. Search for added value.
- See to it that you have sufficient leeway in your bargaining.
- Only bargain with people who are authorized to make decisions.
- Find out all of the other party's demands and preferences before you make an offer.
- Avoid making one-sided concessions. Always require concessions by the other party as a condition for making concessions of your own.
- Be careful to compute things properly.
- Learn to be able answer with a definite "no."
- Remember that making a compromise does not mean dividing things up 50/50.
- Take time to consider things carefully before making any final agreement.

Negotiating effectively involves effective communication

The successful outcome of any negotiations is based to a very great extent on the ability of the parties to communicate with each other. If negotiations are to function properly, there needs to be two-way communication and genuine dialogue. In watching video films of hundreds of negotiations, I have discovered that the major cause of negotiations breaking down and the parties failing to reach agreement is simply a lack of effective communication. Often, those involved had good intentions and were not in serious conflict with one another initially, but failed to understand each other properly.

Poor communication creates conflicts that were not there from the start. The parties misunderstand each other, become suspicious of one another, and fail to communicate openly. This prevents cooperation from developing.

One-way communication

With one-way communication, one party often uses a flood of words to put the other party at a disadvantage and criticizes the other party's position without being open to counter-arguments. False allegations, lies and threats become mixed with one another. Answering questions the other party has raised is avoided. Neither party shows an appreciable interest in the needs or problems on which the demands, desires and aims of the other party are based. An atmosphere of uncertainty, tension and stress develops, and emotions take charge.

The negotiator can be faced here with making the classic decision between fight or flight. The parties either get nowhere at all or invest their energy in battling incessantly. No search for added value takes place.

Many negotiators lack insight into how negotiations are affected by one-way versus two-way communication. They are unaware of how they themselves communicate. Their distrust of the other party discourages any open dialogue. They negotiate as though opening up would lead to an automatic loss. Negotiations easily become long and drawn out, the same arguments being repeated again and again.

Two-way communication

With two-way communication, you listen attentively, ask questions frequently and summarize from time to time what has been said. Asking questions is partly to be certain that the picture you have of what the other party is saying agrees with what he is actually trying to communicate. You also ask questions when you fail to understand, when you are uncertain about things or want more information, or when you want to test ideas. Questions lead to answers. Under such conditions a higher degree of openness and trust develops. Cooperative solutions are found which leave both parties feeling satisfied. Instead of the parties using their energy primarily to fight each other, they direct their attention to matters that can lead to added value being found that both parties can share.

Nevertheless, complete openness is not desirable here. The negotiator who lays all his cards on the table is naive and exposes himself unnecessarily. He is easily exploited. This can lead to his missing out on the added value that is created. In preparing to negotiate, you should decide what information to keep for yourself, and what information to share with the other party.

Failure to be specific or to come up with new ideas

For negotiations to function properly, there should be an ongoing flow of ideas. New information and new perspectives need to be considered. If all of this stops, the agenda that was planned will flop, negotiations will go nowhere, and those involved will simply engage in a battle of words involving the repetition of arguments that the other party scarcely listens to. Arguments also often become increasingly vague and less to the point, as exemplified by such statements as the following: "That would cost too much." "We can't manage it in such a short time." "You'll have to give us better guarantees than that."

Under conditions such as these, both parties have a hard time judging where the truth is in the arguments presented by the other side. These often represent simply a search for opportunities and a test of the strength of an individual's negotiating position. They are elements in a game in which each side takes a tough approach and attempts to badger the other side into giving in. If the arguments the parties exploit are to be believed, they need to be tied to concrete facts and relationships. Both parties need to explain what they mean and why they are making the demands they do. Unless this is done or something new is introduced, negotiations end up in a deadlock.

If negotiations do become deadlocked, you can or may do any of the following things:

- Increase the intensity of your arguments in an effort to persuade the other party, or get the other party to give up. If you are lucky or very skillful, this may work, but the risk is considerable that pressure on your part will increase pressure from the other side, making the deadlock worse. Negotiations come to revolve around matters of prestige. It is not a question simply of what price or whatever is best, but of who is strongest and toughest. Which side will win? Will a party that is hit hard strike back?
- Give in on some point. This gets you out of the deadlock, but sends out the wrong signals, unless you make it completely clear that you are only giving up on that point to make it easier to reach an overall agreement. If the other party does not believe this, you run the risk of regretting the concession. The other party may also now regard you as weak, encouraging him to use further deadlocks to get you to cave in on other points as well.
- If time is running out and there are alternative solutions (sellers, buyers or products) that seem just as good, you can indicate to the other party that you will turn to these if he does not start singing a different tune. If you present this in no uncertain terms, the other party may understand what is in store and decide to give up on the point in question. On the other hand, he may fail to grasp that you are serious and think you are trying to bluff. Threats often lead either party to thinking only in terms of winning or losing, to a complete breakdown of negotiations, or to the other party doubting that the threat is for real. Thus, he may escalate his efforts at getting you to agree, and perhaps present a threat of some

sort himself to get you to reveal where you stand. Questions of prestige tend to come to the fore.
- You can postpone any decisions to be made. Unless you are running out of time, this will give you some breathing space and a chance to sleep on things. However, sometimes postponements make things worse. If you continue postponing things, either you or the other party may find that time has become so short that expectations have to be lowered and both may lose.
- You can come up with something new that clarifies matters better, or points out other solutions that are possible. Two-way communication is very important here, promoting cooperation.
- You can ask questions to cast light on various matters. It is important not to consider demands the other party makes as threats. If you can gain insight into the needs and problems that are behind the other party's demands, this can open up new opportunities for finding solutions. Lack of information needed to keep negotiations going may be due to cowardice or distrust, both on your part and that of the other party. If neither of you opens up for fear of being taken advantage of, and both of you want if possible to get everything, you chances of concluding anything realistic or reasonable are limited.

If you want the other party to open up, you should be ready to take the first step yourself. Do not demand that the other party lay his cards on the table before you are ready to show yours. Dare to live by the golden rule of only asking of others what you demand of yourself. Do not be so naive, however, as to believe that you can be completely open. A buyer that starts off negotiations by telling the supplier that he is searching desperately for a new supplier because the old supplier's factory has burned down, for example, is likely to pay dearly for this.

Acceptable reasons for information flow being one-sided

If one party is supplying the other with information the whole time, without getting any appreciable amount in return, the party providing information may eventually become irritated, feeling he is being used and placed at a disadvantage. This can lead to an emotional exchange that results in negotiations coming to a standstill. The party that has been providing most of the information may want to throw the other party out and break things off for good, saying "We're getting nowhere. You're only pumping us for information without giving us anything."

Breakdowns in communication of this sort can be avoided by letting each other know from the start how you want negotiations to be conducted, and by providing each other with an agenda. This might make temporary one-sided information flows acceptable to both parties.

We tend to be self-centered

We tend to be self-centered and to see negotiations largely from our own standpoint only, feeling that if the other party does not understand, it is his fault. It is easier to blame the other party for everything. By simplifying matters in our own mind, we are able to justify not taking a critical look at our own behavior.

To be successful, you must be willing to recognize your own responsibility for overcoming problems. Whose fault is it if things do not work out? It is your own. If the other party does not listen to what you are saying or aiming at, you should try communicating in some other way. If you do not get answers to your questions, you should stop and reflect, then go on, explaining yourself better. Far too often, we are ready to accept incomprehensible or evasive answers to our questions, or statements, that seem to be pure nonsense. We fail to listen attentively to what the other party says, and we also keep our mouths shut far too often when we should say what we are thinking. Are there factors in our upbringing that hold us back, or is it a lack of insight into how people communicate that leads to our inability or unwillingness to make ourselves understood properly?

A negotiator should never simply behave passively, leaving it up to the other party to clarify what he means. To my dismay, I meet buyers again and again who declare that, if a seller does not succeed in getting a contract, he has only himself to blame. Such buyers feel that, if they have a sufficient number of sellers to choose from, they are not dependent on the individual seller in any way. The buyer indeed has the responsibility of communicating clearly, ensuring that negotiations are constructive.

Wrongly assuming that you know what the other party wants

Example

Late one fall I went to a vaccination center to get a shot for the flu. When my turn came up, the nurse asked me,

> "What can I do for you?"
> "I want the influenza vaccine."
> "Follow me. I'll give you one."

I followed her into the treatment room, where she asked me to take off my trousers. I was somewhat surprised at this and said,

> "But shouldn't I get the shot in my arm?"
> "No, it's always your leg we put it in."
> "But it's always been my arm when I've been here before."
> "Let's get your pants down. We have to get on with things here. We have a waiting room full of patients."

The nurse, persistent and assertive as she was, got me to pull my trousers down and she gave me the shot. When I paid her, I asked for a receipt. The receipt read, "1 shot gamma globulin, $11.25."

> "Why did you give me gamma globulin? I was supposed to get the influenza vaccine."
> "No, you said gamma globulin. You are planning to take a trip."
> "I'm not traveling anywhere, and I said 'influenza vaccine'."
> "But I thought you said gamma globulin."
> "Didn't you react when I told you twice that I'm accustomed to getting it in my arm?"
> "Yes, I thought that was strange."
> "Well would you mind just giving me the influenza vaccine."

She asked me to wait while she went out.
    She came back five minutes later and said,

"You won't be getting a shot for the flu today. When you've gotten gamma globulin, you have to wait at least three weeks before you can have a flu shot."

Upset by all of this, I asked to get my $11.25 back, but she refused, saying I had after all gotten a shot of gamma globulin. She said I could get a flu shot for free three weeks later if I did not get one somewhere else.

We hear and see what we want to. We anticipate from the start how things will be and guard ourselves against information to the contrary. Although "gamma globulin" and "influenza vaccine" both do end with an "in" or "een" sound, the two are not at all alike in other respects. Since the nurse somehow thought that I was to go off on a trip, she was certain it was gamma globulin I was supposed to get.

Routinely summarizing what has been said

How can misunderstandings of this sort be avoided? To do so, make use of a procedure that is used in military operations, that of requesting the other party to repeat what has just been said. Suppose that in negotiating with three people who make up the other party you suggest a certain modification to an idea they have just suggested. They find that your counter-suggestion is interesting and ask for a 15-minute break to go out and discuss things with each other. Think how foolish it would be, though, if they had not understood your suggestion properly and ended up discussing something different. Suppose that just before they decided to ask for a break you said the following to them:

Example
"I like your suggestion of doing things jointly, and I think we can go along with the sharing of responsibility, as well as the work and risks involved. But I'd suggest we come to some other arrangement regarding profits. Since we're talking about cooperation, it doesn't seem quite right to me that you pay us for what we've done and then go out and sell it all to your customers. I think we should share the profits on a 40/60 basis."
"That's a different arrangement from what we had in mind. I

won't say we can't go along with the idea, but could you wait a quarter of an hour while the three of us go out and discuss the matter?"

The members of the other party go out and begin discussing things:

"Let's see how large the net earnings might be."
"Net earnings? Why should we compute that?
"We'd be sharing the profits."
"Yes, but profits and net earnings aren't the same thing."
"What are the profits, then?

Their discussion continues and they manage to end up with a basically correct interpretation of what you meant by "profits." They compute the sum this could be expected to amount to and determine what 40 percent of that would be. If they had been asked later to explain why they accepted a profit of only 40 percent, they might respond with the following:

"Their negotiator suggested we get 40 percent."
"Is that really what he said?"
"Yes, the exact words were, 'We should share the profits on a 40/60 basis.'"
"And who did he intend should get the 40 and the 60?"
"We'd get 40 percent."
"That's not what he said."
"Yes he did, he said we'd share the profits on a 40/60 basis.'"

In reality, what you had meant was that they should get 60 percent of the profits.

Avoid the risk of such misunderstandings by always asking the other party to summarize any suggestions you have made. In this case, you could have said, "Before you go out, could you give me a quick summary of what I've suggested to make sure I've expressed myself clearly?"

If you do this consistently, you will be rather surprised at how many times others misunderstand you, and at how unclearly you sometimes express yourself. Asking for a summary provides an opportunity to correct any false impressions you may have given. Also, when you listen to the other party's summary, you can sometimes detect from their choice of words or manner of speaking what their attitude is toward your suggestion, and to what extent they might accept it.

Another important lesson here is that you should not be satisfied with simply making a suggestion. You should also perform whatever computations are necessary, and show the other party how things would work and what they would be getting. Similarly, if you get a suggestion from the other party, ask to see things worked out so that you will know what the suggestion entails.

To simply ask without doing all of this is dangerous. Determine whether the two of you agree, whether the other party has understood your point, and whether he thinks it will even work. Ask such questions as: "Could you explain how you think this would work?"; "What would that mean for you in monetary terms?"; "What is it that we've agreed on?"

An important technique for ensuring clear communication is to make ample use of the words who, what, when, where, how and why. Develop a personal practice of using these terms as part of your routine summary of what has been arrived. Do this before moving on to the next point on the agenda. Make sure both parties contribute to these summaries.

Preparing written summaries

The idea for both parties in negotiating is to reach an agreement that leads to the signing of a contract. Wishful thinking and jumping to conclusions, however, can sometimes lead both parties into thinking they have agreed when they really have not. I have often seen negotiators saying at the close of negotiations, "We've now reached an agreement on things," only to discover a short time later that they differ in their conception of what the agreement means and its implications. Part of the reason for this could be that no summaries were ever made, or that there were too few. However, it could also be that the summaries themselves were not clear enough.

In any negotiations that are important and result in an agreement, both parties should have had a common written version of the agreement and have been of the same opinion regarding meanings and interpretations. A summary document can do much to prevent future misunderstandings and disputes.

Kjell Olof Feldt, Finance Minister of Sweden (1982 to 1990), has described how he and Prime Minister Olof Palme (1969 to 1976 and 1982 to 1986), failed to maintain any written summary of what was agreed upon during negotiations conducted in 1985 with the Swedish labor unions. There were no official documents concerning measures taken and promises made, or by whom. Accordingly, the various parties involved differed in their interpretations of the oral agreements reached, resulting in failed negotiations, which allowed wages and inflation in Sweden to climb out of control. Kjell Olof Feldt said that Olof Palme and he wanted intensely to demonstrate that the wage policies achieved by the Swedish government through negotiations were successful. For this very reason, they decided against putting the agreements that were made down in writing, being afraid that, if they did, the agreements might not hold. It was as if they wanted only to believe that they were completely successful and that full agreement had been reached, whereas in fact this was not the case.

The mistake of trying to avoid conflict at all costs

Some people dislike conflict so much they try to avoid it at all costs. They "beat around the bush" instead of meeting sensitive issues head on. As a result, what they want, or where they stand, is never made clear. This makes communication difficult and ineffective.

Example
The following negotiations took place early one year between the head of a small company and a member of its staff. It was a company that for the past 20 years had always closed down in July, when everyone went on vacation. The staff member in question came in to his boss and asked,

> "What would you say if I took some of my vacation during September this year?"
> "I'm not sure what I'd say about that...we always close down in July...but, apart from that, I don't know what I'd say."

"That sounds good. Have you heard, by the way, whether we've gotten an order in from Denmark?"

Their conversation soon turns to other things. Several months go by. At the end of August the staff member meets his boss in the hallway and says,

"Since we won't be seeing each other for some time, I just wanted to say goodbye before I take off."
"Yes, where are you off to?"
"To Greece."
"To Greece? Are we doing business there?"
"No, I'll be spending three weeks there on vacation."
"Three weeks! What do you mean? Taking off in September now when we have so much to do? Why didn't you spend your vacation there in July? You can't take off now."
"We discussed this with each other at the beginning of the year and we agreed that it was all right. You can't go back on an agreement the two of us made."
"We didn't make any agreement."

A real conflict was in the making. Both of them were equally surprised and irreconcilable. Each of them was agitated and sure he was right. They became so emotionally wrought that it was difficult for them to think clearly about the problem. Who was in the right and who was in the wrong? Both of them, in fact, were equally responsible for what happened. What was it then that had happened at the start, back in January?

The staff member had formulated his request in a vague way, since he was afraid of being rebuffed. He had opened by asking, "What would you say if I took *some* of my vacation during September...?" He had been afraid to express himself clearly, which would have entailed mentioning a three-week vacation. His boss had heard what he said, but got the impression that the employee was uncertain about things. Rather than rebuke his request, he had avoided making any clear decision, thus avoiding conflict. The answer he had given was nothing short of pure gibberish. What had he really meant?

Here the staff member should have stopped and asked himself,

"What's he trying to say? Does he mean that I can or that I can't take a vacation in September?" He should have seen to it that he got a clear answer, summarizing then what his boss had said to ensure mutual understanding. The employee might have stated, "We've agreed then that there's no difficulty in my..." His boss, in turn, should not have allowed him to simply change the subject as he did by asking about an order from Denmark. He should have stopped things by asking,

> "Are we clear about this matter of your vacation?"
> "Yes."
> "What was it we agree about?"

Here he would have forced the staff member to summarize the agreement that supposedly had been reached. Since indeed no agreement had been arrived at, it quickly would have become clear to both of them that a misunderstanding was in the making. Instead of postponing the clarification, potentially allowing this serious conflict to develop, the two of them should have discussed openly where they stood, allowing them to agree on a solution that both of them could have accepted.

Too often we communicate using only one medium

Although many negotiating situations offer you access to more than one medium for presenting information to a group – such as an overhead, a slide projector, a whiteboard, paper and pencil, or whatever – too little use is made of these. Many negotiators simply sit in their chair attempting to explain everything orally, even when explaining complex ideas involving the computation of large figures with many steps. Without something for others to see, presentations of this sort can be very difficult to comprehend.

Researchers have shown that up to twice as much material can be communicated successfully if your oral presentation includes visual material, such as photos, diagrams or lists of key words. If you listen to a radio weather report for a large geographical area and attempt to recall what you have heard, you may end up only being able to remember the weather prediction for the area where you are. If you look at a comparable weather report on TV, where you are provided with two mediums of information, it is much easier to see how things are related and you are likely to recall much more.

Presenting negative matters in the right way

It is important to express yourself as clearly as possible. To this end, you should not focus merely on what and how you are saying things. You need to pay close attention to whether the other party understands you. Be conscious of how they interpret what you are saying, and adjust to their way of understanding. Being open and honest, when appropriate, does help, and how you proceed can be very important. If the message you convey is negative in character, the other party may perceive you as a threat and consider it impossible to negotiate. He may go on the defensive to protect himself in various ways, such as simply closing his ears to what you are saying. If you present things too suddenly or in too direct a manner, the risk for this increases. It is better in this situation to begin by providing certain background information so he can understand things in basically the same way as you.

Example
A husband arrives home after shopping for furniture:

> "I saw a fantastic sofa today. It was perfect for our living room. It's high time we threw out the old one. I brought a brochure with me. Look how nice it is."

> One answer the spouse might give is: "But it costs $3,500. We don't have money to squander on that sort of thing."

How it went on from there you can imagine.

> However, the spouse could have chosen a different approach: "It really looks nice. But do you know what we got in the mail today? The interest on our loan is going to be increased by 1.5 percent. That'll cost us $2,250 extra a year."

> "Do you think the couch would be too expensive then?"
> "Well, we could buy it if we economize on something else."

Additional problems in communicating effectively

There is no possible way to list all the basic communication problems you might run across in negotiating, but here are some examples of what to watch for:

- A person's body and mouth speaking different languages.
- Communicating from different cultures.
- Communicating under time pressure.
- Communication where parties do not treat each other as equals.
- Use of communication tactics that intend to manipulate or create uncertainty.

Summary of communication

- Avoid one-way communication.
- Ask questions and summarize what has been said. Be sure to get clear answers to your questions. Check whether you have reached an agreement and what has been agreed upon.
- Provide the information needed for negotiations to succeed. Realize that, to be trusted, you need to be open in communicating with the other party.
- Listen to the other party. Remember that constructive arguments are most effective when they relate to the other party's needs and interests.
- Realize that, if the other party does not understand, the fault is yours.
- Do not assume that you know what the other party wants to say. Avoid 'seeing' and 'hearing' only what you want to see and hear.
- Remember to ask the other party to summarize, allowing you to check for misunderstandings.
- Prepare together with the other party a written summary of all important agreements.
- Do not forget to use the words *who, what, when, where, why* and *how.*
- Avoid expressing yourself in any unclear manner.
- Use visual aids to help clarify your oral message.
- Present matters of negative character in the right way, giving the other party sufficient background information first.

Estimating your negotiating power

Suppose you want a higher salary. You know that you are important to your company, and that other companies would be ready to hire you for a higher salary. You go to your boss and say:

> **Example**
> "I've just been offered a job at another company. Actually, I don't want to quit, but they're offering me $3,750 a month instead of the $3,000 I'm earning here. It would be difficult for me to turn down $750 a month. What do you think I should do?"
> "Take the job," he says. "You can clean off your desk and go at the end of the month."

Learn a lesson from this. Do not overestimate the strength of your negotiating position. It is likely that your boss will have priorities different from yours. He must take into account the fact that any agreement he makes with you can establish a precedent. Do not give your boss an ultimatum of the type exemplified here if you do not have a genuine alternative.

> **Example**
> Suppose the Department of Highways intends to build a new road that cuts across your property and wants, therefore, to buy a piece of your property. You oppose the building of such a road, but no one listens to you. You finally understand that you can prevent neither the building of the road nor its cutting across your property. You have fought the matter all the way and now the Department of Highways is getting impatient with you. They threaten to file an application to expropriate your property. You certainly want to avoid this, being uncertain about the economic consequences this would have, yet you feel you are being taken advantage of by the government and its bureaucrats.
> You ask yourself whether there may be certain hidden opportunities. You consider that such an expropriation would cost the

Department of Highways a considerable sum of money. In addition to legal expenses, it would be a considerable amount of time before the case appeared in court. Such a delay in construction would add to their costs. So you come to what seems like a perfectly logical conclusion, which is that the Department would save a lot of money by reaching a quick settlement with you instead of pursuing the expropriation. Even if you see no chance of stopping the road from being built across your property, you can at least try to get a good price for it.

The Department does not have to view things that way at all, however. What consequences would it have if you managed to get a really generous settlement in this way? This could encourage other property owners in similar situations to pursue the same delay strategy. What could the Department be expected to do to prevent this? In order to indicate to property owners that it is not worthwhile to delay things in this way, they could be expected to make it a policy of only providing generous settlements to people who agreed early.

Thus, the strength of your position may not always be as great as it appears.

The importance of chemistry in how people interact

Often, whether a contract is signed will depend more on interpersonal chemistry than on rational factors such as price or performance. Experienced negotiators emphasize how important personal relationships are. When doing business with someone, you should try to become acquainted with him, partly in an attempt to determine what sort of person he is. Whether you decide to do business with this person again often depends on how much confidence and trust you have developed.

Social interactions are regulated not only by written, but also by unwritten laws, deeply embedded in a person's culture. In some companies, a social blunder that you inadvertently commit can prevent a business relationship from developing, whereas in other companies there is much greater tolerance for mistakes of this sort.

Emotional signals

The book by the well-known PR man, Mark McCormack, *What They Don't Teach You at Harvard Business School,* deals basically with a single theme: how to achieve good interpersonal chemistry in business situations. How people interact is very much a function of transmitted social signals.

Such signals carry many types of messages. They may say to others that your aim is to inform, to influence, to impress, to manipulate, to protest, or whatever. Some signals are conscious ones you can clearly express and others are ones you may scarcely be aware of, or know nothing about. The party you direct signals at usually understands at least some of your signals, and either misunderstands or fails to understand others. Much of the interaction between two people consists of the exchange of signals that reflect emotional reactions. Unless this exchange of emotional signals functions smoothly and rapidly, allowing people to get on the same wavelength and do so quickly, communication becomes ineffective. If the emotional signals a person sends out are hard to interpret, or if he easily misinterprets or is slow in reacting to the emotional signals sent by others, his communication with others will often be ineffective.

Reacting to emotional signals can sometimes go too far

When the exchange of emotional signals between two people is particularly effective, the danger may exist for one or both of them to be so strongly influenced by this that making rational decisions becomes difficult. If the signals are of a positive character, one or both of them may experience the situation as being so positive that decisions become based more on feelings than on facts.

This can be exemplified by negotiations that took place in Sweden in January of 1986 between P.G. Gyllenhammar, head of Volvo, and Refaat El-Sayed, an Egyptian businessman who a year before had bought Fermenta, a firm that manufactured penicillin, purchasing it from Astra, a large Swedish pharmaceutical company. Since Volvo was a major stockholder in the Swedish pharmaceutical firm Pharmacia, the idea of Volvo making a deal with a pharmaceutical firm was not at all out of the ordinary. During the year El-Sayed had been in control of Fermenta, its stocks had risen like a rocket, with Fermenta becoming one of the 16 most highly traded stocks on the Swedish stock market. Within an extremely short period of time negotiations were conducted between Volvo and Fermenta, resulting in a contract between the two companies, to the considerable astonishment of the public. Gyllenhammar called the signing of this contract one of the most important developments of the decade in the Swedish business world. Gyllenhammar explained the speed with which negotiations went so quickly by saying, *"Such things should be done fast if both parties feel that their thoughts and ideas coincide."* Afterwards, knowing what happened, one can clearly see that things went too fast. El-Sayed had bluffed. Fermenta was a house of cards. The agreement with Fermenta ended up costing Volvo some $3,125,000, and El-Sayed went to prison for six years. Fermenta stocks sank to a tenth of what their value had been.

In his book *Also with Feelings*, published by Bonniers in 1991, Gyllenhammar commented on this agreement with Fermenta. He introduced a chapter on the subject with the following words: *My wife has* *often said to me that I'm naive and make a thousand mistakes...That may well be true. Perhaps I am naive and surely I'm impulsive. If I hit upon an idea I'm fascinated by, I can get wildly excited about it...The Fermenta agreement...didn't come about as suddenly as has often been claimed...We were already open to the idea of structural changes in this area when Refaat El-Sayed appeared on the scene. We didn't know much more about this creation of his than what had been said and written about it publicly. Han-*delsbanken (a major bank in Sweden) *helped fill us in on some of the de-*tails... *We became one of the many victims, though this doesn't lessen the need one has to drawing one's own conclusions about things...I first met Refaat El-Sayed at the end of 1986...I was fascinated by the plan... he presented. Volvo was to be one of the major owners in this new organization that was to be created, and it was to be the dominant party in the long run. I liked the idea. We met again shortly thereafter...The arrangement was a simple one and easy to grasp...We were pushed somewhat into going ahead and confirming that there was a sketch of this plan...Before the ink had dried on the basic agreement on principles we signed, a schism had already developed...There was an uproar about his having lied about his back-ground...I was still ready to believe what he had said... The next day it was shown that he had lied...When anything of this sort happens, it opens your eyes and you take a much more careful look at things.*

Clothing

Your choice of clothing sends out various signals. In a broad sense, your clothing also includes such things as your wristwatch, your briefcase, and the car you drive. Clothing tends to show what group you belong to and your economic status. It sends out signals readily interpreted as reflecting your personality, showing you to be sloppy, neat, unkempt, organized, exhibitionistic, modest, receptive, unreceptive, boring, colorful, correct, elegant or whatever.

Consultants offering advice on how people can create a positive image of themselves are in demand today. The need for use of such consultants is due to the problem that many people create negative images of themselves by sending out the wrong signals, many of which involve exterior appearance.

Why is clothing so important? It sends a signal, and is therefor part of our language. Clothing tells others how successful we are, and the extent to which we feel we should follow social norms and conventions. We can either accept existing clothing norms or demonstrate our rejection of them. The latter basically amounts, however, to changing from one uniform to another, and in this sense the person in question may be just as formal as before. Earlier rules of etiquette are simply replaced by new ones. These, though not formalized in writing, may be stricter than those from earlier. Whatever the situation, if you oppose existing norms, you are in danger of being misunderstood.

Body language

Many of the signals about yourself that are conveyed to others represent a kind of body language. Such signals can create either a positive or a negative impression. Certain negative signals are fully within our power to avoid, such as a feeble handshake, avoiding eye contact, a slouched stance, speaking in a low voice, invading someone else's space, disagreeable body odors and bad breath. Positive and negative body language signals to consider would be far too innumerable to list. Air-hostesses for SAS are trained to look passengers in the eye, to gain a passenger's attention by laying a hand gently on their arm, and to call passengers by their first name. This provides a personal touch and makes a positive impression on behalf of the airline.

Everybody is different – accepting yourself and others

You should never delude yourself into thinking you can change other people. The only person you might be able to change, with considerable effort, is yourself. Such an endeavor cannot be accomplished overnight. Being a successful negotiator does not require you to behave out of character or pretending to be someone you are not. An artificial portrayal of yourself will eventually become transparent, and in many situations it will have just the opposite effect from what you intend. Try to see the interactions taking place at the negotiating table through the eyes of others. Ask yourself which of your characteristics are evident here. To what extent are they to my advantage or my disadvantage?

That which in one situation contributes positively to that particular group chemistry may have just the opposite effect elsewhere. Since a given contribution of yours could cause things to go well in one negotiating situation and poorly in another, pay close attention and do not become complacent with yourself. Try to identify the types of signals you send out that people in general, or even specific individuals, react either positively or negatively to.

Social skills and sensitivity to the needs and interests of others are important. You should treat others as you wish to be treated, and respect them for who they are. All of this will help you avoid unnecessary conflicts.

How good a listener are you? Do you really listen to what the other party is saying, or do you simply wait anxiously for him to finish so that you can have your say? If you demonstrate that you are listening to the other party and understand him, this will increase the chances that he will listen to you.

Do you know enough about your business partners' personal interests, ideas, views, family relationships and cultural background to be able to avoid saying the wrong things? Matters such as these are not always easy to find out. Everyone has some limits as to how close he will allow others can come. Some people prefer keeping you at a distance. Others are more open to revealing themselves. Whatever the situation, attempting to force matters will only cause problems.

Be ready to engage in small talk

When negotiating, it is often a bad strategy to attempt getting into things too fast. You should first get to know the other party, unless you know him well already. It is important to establish a sense of trust and give the other party the chance to relax and feel in a good mood.

Those at the negotiating table should devote some time to small talk – about local, national or world events, about themselves, or anything else of interest to those present. They should have something to eat or drink and should feel at home. The Swedish diplomat Gunnar Jarring said once in an interview, "There are two characteristics a skillful diplomat should possess. One is that he should be able to go on indefinitely talking about the weather. The other is that he should be able to go on indefinitely without saying a thing."

You must obviously get to the task at hand, but moving slowly in the beginning is often a good approach.

Becoming a better negotiator

As has been shown, negotiations are a kind of game that people frequently engage in. Everyone involved and every task with which negotiators are faced is unique. Your own personal characteristics and beliefs will be important building blocks for achieving a good solution to the problems you deal with. To succeed as a negotiator, you have to believe in what you are doing. If you also enjoy negotiating and feel it is exciting, this will be much to your advantage.

It is my sincere hope that my personal experiences, shared with you in these pages, will help you along the way, but they will never suffice to make you a full-fledged negotiator. You will need training and practice, which can best be achieved by engaging in negotiations frequently and profiting from what each new case has to teach you. Over time, you will acquire the skills and confidence needed to firmly take the bold steps that are often called for.

I wish you success in your continued efforts to be a good negotiator.